Collegial Coaching

Collegial Coaching

Mentoring for Knowledge and Skills That Transfer to Real-World Applications

Katie Alaniz

ROWMAN & LITTLEFIELD
Lanham • Boulder • New York • London

Published by Rowman & Littlefield
An imprint of The Rowman & Littlefield Publishing Group, Inc.
4501 Forbes Boulevard, Suite 200, Lanham, Maryland 20706
www.rowman.com

86-90 Paul Street, London EC2A 4NE, United Kingdom

Copyright © 2022 by Katie Alaniz

All rights reserved. No part of this book may be reproduced in any form or by any electronic or mechanical means, including information storage and retrieval systems, without written permission from the publisher, except by a reviewer who may quote passages in a review.

British Library Cataloguing in Publication Information Available

Library of Congress Cataloging-in-Publication Data

Names: Alaniz, Katie, author.
Title: Collegial coaching : mentoring for knowledge and skills that transfer to real-world applications / Katie Alaniz.
Description: Lanham : Rowman & Littlefield, [2022] | Includes bibliographical references. | Summary: "The book details the process of collegial coaching within school environments, focusing upon content-specific goals and objectives, sound instructional strategies, and authentic assessment opportunities"— Provided by publisher.
Identifiers: LCCN 2021032111 (print) | LCCN 2021032112 (ebook) | ISBN 9781475860306 (cloth) | ISBN 9781475860313 (paperback) | ISBN 9781475860320 (epub)
Subjects: LCSH: Mentoring in education. | Career development. | Educational technology.
Classification: LCC LB1731.4 .A43 2022 (print) | LCC LB1731.4 (ebook) | DDC 371.102—dc23
LC record available at https://lccn.loc.gov/2021032111
LC ebook record available at https://lccn.loc.gov/2021032112

This book is dedicated to the glory of God and to the memory of Dr. Dawn K. Wilson, a cherished teacher, mentor, and friend.

Contents

Preface: Why the Coaching CPR Framework for Innovative Learning? ... ix

Acknowledgments ... xv

Introduction ... xvii

1 Resuscitating Professional Development with Collegial Coaching ... 1
2 Coaches to the Rescue in an Age of Rapid Response ... 15
3 Deploying the Coaching CPR Model ... 27
4 First Responders of Professional Development ... 47
5 The Urgency of Content-Focused Coaching ... 61
6 The Life-Giving Power of Purposeful Pedagogy ... 69
7 Reviving Learning through Authentic Assessment ... 83

Conclusion ... 95

About the Author ... 103

Preface

Why the Coaching CPR Framework for Innovative Learning?

The inspiration for writing this guidebook developed as a result of numerous shared experiences. I first encountered the opportunity to serve as a collegial coaching during my time as a master of education student at Houston Baptist University in Houston, Texas. The experience was designed and supervised by Dr. Dawn Wilson, the developer of the MEd in curriculum and instruction with a specialization in instructional technology program offered through the university.

DR. WILSON'S JOURNEY

In 2006, Dr. Bill Borgers, a perceptive and forward-thinking dean of the College of Education and Behavioral Science at Houston Baptist University, hired Dr. Wilson to serve as the college's technology integration specialist. As a former school superintendent, Dr. Borgers perceived an impending shift of the educational landscape and observed that his faculty was falling behind in technological knowledge and skills. He recognized that the faculty, while exceptional face-to-face instructors, lacked a firm grasp of the digital proficiencies needed to fully prepare current and future educators.

Dr. Borgers initially appointed Dr. Wilson to direct the College of Education faculty in incorporating technology within their classes. Over time, as her work proved tremendously effective with the faculty in her own college, Dr. Wilson began supporting instructors from across the university in various departments. She invested significant time in one-on-one support of colleagues, guiding them in closing gaps in knowledge and skills and individually heightening faculty members' expertise and confidence. Dr. Wilson devoted time with colleagues in their offices, helping them as they designed digital presentations, incorporated videos, and constructed their own professional technical repertoire in a multitude of additional ways.

Serving alongside these content area experts proved to be a life-altering experience. Dr. Wilson encountered firsthand that highly knowledgeable and skilled educators often require differentiated support to surmount their personal fears and inexperience with regard to technology integration in the classroom. The assurance of having a colleague available for answers and support bridged the digital divide for many of these faculty members. Dr. Wilson, herself a former public school teacher of sixteen years, shared a collective pedagogy with her higher education colleagues, thus connecting them as they together considered, selected, and implemented effective instructional strategies.

Not only did she impart her technological expertise to faculty, but Dr. Wilson also facilitated a technology course for graduate students—and, in time, for undergraduate preservice teachers—at the university. Understandably, some students required more hand-holding than others. Nonetheless, all ultimately designed authentic assessment pieces with various technology tools and resources in preparation to advance as educators in the digital age.

Among many other applications, the students learned to create graphic organizers, develop online portfolios, and design their own instructional videos. As each semester concluded, students consistently remarked on how accomplished they felt because of their learning and application of new knowledge and skills. They seemed consistently eager to showcase the artifacts of learning they had developed. These students undeniably expanded their personal and professional efficiency, which went on to serve them well within classroom settings.

These experiences led to the realization that many teachers do not intentionally resist technology integration; rather, they often need a caring colleague to invest time in helping them on an individual basis, coaching them through the process of effectively incorporating digital tools and resources. They need a coach to guide them from the start of their integration work. Teachers benefit from the help of a colleague who refuses to give up on their growth, offers consistent feedback, and keeps them accountable until they eventually incorporate technology in meaningful ways for their students.

Ultimately, this experience introduced an exceptional means by which to heighten teachers' expertise with technology integration. While the technology tools and course design have changed over time, Dr. Wilson spent the remainder of her days embracing opportunities to facilitate effective technology integration alongside numerous educators, semester after semester, in schools across the city of Houston and beyond.

DR. ALANIZ'S JOURNEY

My experience differs significantly from Dr. Wilson's. Through my time spent teaching first and second grade for close to a decade in both public and private school settings, I often observed heightened student engagement and enthusiasm for learning when digital tools and resources played a role in classroom activities. Desiring to more effectively leverage the opportunities provided by instructional technology, I pursued a Master of Education in Curriculum and Instruction with a specialization in Instructional Technology at Houston Baptist University.

Under Dr. Wilson's leadership of this program, I became progressively more aware of the immense array of digital tools and resources available for enhancing learners' educational experiences. Following each graduate class session, I sought to incorporate the novel technological skills I learned within my second grade classroom, and I quickly discovered that my students unfailingly reacted with tremendous enthusiasm.

For example, my second graders intently viewed a claymation video I designed to support my students in grasping the cardinal directions in social studies. At the video's conclusion, my young learners responded with a heartfelt round of applause. Moments such as this occurred repeatedly during my graduate program, consistently enhancing my confidence in the power of meaningfully implemented instructional technology. These instances provided me with heightened resolve to uncover additional innovative means of integrating technology in classroom settings.

Furthermore, such experiences inspired me to seek out opportunities to support colleagues in more effectively incorporating instructional technology within their own instructional endeavors. Incidentally, my graduate program included a highly influential course taught by Dr. Wilson on collegial coaching for technology integration.

Through this course, my classmates and I each conferenced with three colleagues within our school settings, coaching them in incorporating technology into their daily instructional contexts in identified areas of need. This experience ultimately sparked my belief in the power of coaching for positively influencing educators' use of technological tools. Through the process of discovering, designing, and implementing various digital tools and resources with coached teachers, I observed the effectiveness of coaching on a firsthand basis.

After completing my master of education degree and beginning a doctoral program focusing upon learning, design, and technology, I became a part-time teacher at a private school in the Houston area. As I contemplated various research interests, I felt naturally drawn to studying the potential of coaching to spark enhanced reflective practices—this time focusing upon student teachers. Serving shoulder-to-shoulder alongside hundreds of burgeoning educators as they reflected on their growth as future teachers, I again observed the impact of coaching within a nonthreatening, peer-to-peer context.

Before my doctoral program commenced, I began serving as a digital learning specialist within my school in addition to my part-time role as an elementary computer instructor. This position provides me with the opportunity to consult with classroom teachers as they seek out innovative methods of technology integration. In doing so, I experience the power of coaching to heighten teachers' motivation and skill as they seek to effectively apply digital tools and resources to classroom contexts.

As a part-time digital learning specialist on my school campus, I collaborate with teachers, supporting them in achieving their goals for leveraging the tools at their disposal. I frequently observe the increased enthusiasm and confidence these educators demonstrate as they seek to grow in a safe, voluntary professional development context.

Inspired and encouraged by Dr. Wilson's example of educational excellence within a higher education setting, I joined the faculty of the College of Education and Behavioral Sciences soon after graduating with my doctoral degree. In this role, I enjoy countless opportunities to implement the coaching practices initially modeled for me by Dr. Wilson over a decade ago in my master of education program.

As fellow educators, Dr. Wilson and I beheld the potential of coaching for enhancing instructional effectiveness, time and time again. The forthcoming chapters were written on the basis of the belief that teachers sincerely want to be innovative educators, knowing that they play a vital role in students' academic success.

IN HONOR OF DR. WILSON . . .

On September 9, 2019, Dr. Wilson passed from this earth to her eternal home after bravely fighting cancer for five years. Through her final moments, she consistently demonstrated remarkable courage, an unfaltering sense of hope, and a unextinguishable passion for her life's calling. She expertly coached colleagues with care and guided her students in accomplishing the same, even in her last days.

Dr. Wilson's life and legacy embody the inspiration for this book. The pages within it serve as a tribute to this truly remarkable educator and genuinely brilliant individual. Those who experienced the light of her presence are infinitely better for having known her.

Acknowledgments

I want to express my profound gratitude to my husband, Steven, and to my family, friends, colleagues, and students for consistently encouraging and supporting me in fulfilling my life's calling.

This book is fully dedicated to the glory of God, and the pages therein have been written in honor of my extraordinary mentor and friend, Dr. Dawn Wilson. If not for Dr. Wilson's invaluable inspiration as my graduate professor, sincere encouragement as my dissertation committee member, wise guidance during my process of transitioning into the world of higher education, and steadfast friendship through every step of the way, this writing of this book, along with countless other professional milestones, would never have come to fruition. Dr. Wilson embodied the ultimate collegial coach, shaping the hearts and minds of students and colleagues for the better and impacting countless souls for eternity. Her brilliance, innovative perspectives, zest for learning, and love for God and others profoundly touched the lives of all who knew her, most certainly including mine.

Not a day goes by in which I fail to think of, and truly miss, Dr. Wilson's remarkable presence. Her life will always be remembered through her teaching and writing, and especially the legacy carried on by those she so lovingly guided and invested in during her time spent on this earth.

"Be strong and courageous. Do not be afraid; do not be discouraged, for the Lord your God will be with you wherever you go." —Joshua 1:9 NIV

Introduction

Whether read from the viewpoint of a district or campus administrator, digital learning specialist, instructional coach, curriculum expert, or other stakeholder supporting educators in maximizing the vast potential of digital tools and resources within classroom settings, this guidebook sheds light upon the boundless promise of collegial coaching for positively impacting student learning experiences. The book commences by familiarizing the reader with the power of knowledge transfer between collegial coaches and coached teachers.

In an age of rapidly expanding digital innovation within educational settings and beyond, professional development targeting content-focused, pedagogically sound, results-based technology integration remains an area of tremendous need. The Coaching CPR Method uniquely fulfills this need. More specifically, it explores the process of collegial coaching within school environments that focuses upon content-specific goals and objectives, aligns with sound instructional strategies, and incorporates authentic assessment opportunities to transform student learning experiences.

Chapter 1 describes the history of collegial coaching within educational settings. Such programs have been recommended as an integral component of comprehensive professional development strategies for aiding teachers in meeting the demands of their occupation. This chapter presents an overview of the literature in support of this model.

Chapter 2 highlights the new dilemmas facing educators guiding today's classrooms. Confronted with increasing demands for accountability—including high-stakes assessments, more stringent regulations, and amplified curricular standards—many teachers are unable to find the time necessary to research the latest digital tools for educational use, let alone determine how to incorporate them into the required curriculum. Support in doing so is needed now more than ever before.

Chapter 3 underscores the significance of a coaching model that focuses upon content-specific goals and objectives, employs solid pedagogical strategies, and targets authentic assessment opportunities. This method provides a professional helping relationship in which a coach with expertise and experience aids the learning and acquisition of new skills by a colleague. This process represents a professional development vehicle by which educators can learn to integrate digital tools with success.

Past research centers specifically upon the process of enhancing collegial coaching for technology integration through the use of the Technological Pedagogical Content Knowledge (TPCK) framework (Mishra, 2008), which later became the TPACK framework (Herring, Koehler, & Mishra, 2016). While the TPACK framework focuses on "the active and constructive teacher," the Coaching CPR Method advocates coaching the teacher toward integrating student-centered approaches using technology as a tool to deliver and transform learning.

Chapter 4 describes the process of creating a collaborative learning environment in which teachers coach teachers. Topics include expanding coaches' background knowledge and skills, exploring principles for effective coaching, and providing structure and ongoing support of coaching processes. This chapter provides strategies and techniques for cultivating quality coaches within school settings.

Chapter 5 details the process of coaching from the perspective of "content as king." While many school districts employ content specialists (or content coaches), they also separately employ instructional technologists. Some even hire instructional coaches whose work is generic in nature, focusing only on pedagogy, as though effective teaching practices transcend content areas. However, there is evidence to support the notion that collegial coaching with an emphasis on content knowledge strengthens teachers' pedagogical practices, particularly those associated with the design and implementation of learning experiences involving digital tools and resources (Alaniz & Wilson, 2015).

Chapter 6 highlights the importance of sound pedagogical practices in coaching for technology integration. Instructional activities are focused so that they support and engage a combination of learning tasks incorporating digital tools to learn with, rather than from. Today's teachers should demonstrate knowledge not only of content but also of pedagogy and technology, and teachers possessing this amalgamation of expertise are few and far between.

Effective coaches must be able to move teachers from just using technology to transforming the learning as a result of technology use. Another key factor in the success of the Coaching CPR Model is the ability to differentiate the coaching to the teachers' needs while moving them from substitution (in the SAMR Model) to augmentation, to modification, and finally to redefinition (Keene, 2015).

Chapter 7 focuses upon the profound impact that results-based coaching methods ultimately have upon student learning. As coaches support teachers in developing authentic learning endeavors, students receive memorable, applicable learning experiences that transfer to the world beyond the walls of the classroom. This chapter introduces an innovative formula for meaningful learning, namely: authentic issues + authentic audiences + authentic assessment = authentic learning experiences. This chapter outlines a plan for guiding teachers in introducing their students to real-world problems to solve, providing them with the opportunity to present solutions to various audiences, and designing assessment endeavors that apply to the everyday lives of learners.

The conclusion comprises a summative overview of fostering an environment of content-focused, pedagogically sound, results-based collegial coaching within school settings. As coached teachers achieve developmental milestones, their enthusiasm often becomes contagious, thus inspiring them to share these successes with their colleagues.

This guidebook concludes with real-life successes involving the transformation of teacher technology integration through the Coaching CPR Method, designed to inspire and inform readers in their journey to implement this strategy within their own professional settings. An investment in this coaching strategy holds the potential to transform the culture of a campus in profound, perpetual ways.

REFERENCES

Alaniz, K., & Wilson, D. (2015). *Naturalizing digital immigrants: The power of collegial coaching for technology integration.* Lanham, MD: Rowman & Littlefield Education.

Herring, M. C., Koehler, M. J., & Mishra, P. (2016). *Handbook of technological pedagogical content knowledge (TPACK) for educators* (2nd ed.). New York, NY: Routledge.

Keene, K. (2015, March 28) *Coaching teachers toward effective technology use: SAMR and TPACK*. Retrieved from http://www.teachintechgal.com/single-post/2015/05/28/Coaching-Teachers-Toward-Effective-Technology-Use-SAMR-TPACK

Mishra, P. (2008). *Handbook of TPCK AACTE Committee on Innovation and Technology*. New York, NY: Routledge.

Chapter One

Resuscitating Professional Development with Collegial Coaching

"Alone we can do so little; together we can do so much."—Helen Keller

Within many educational realms, "business as usual" involves faculty and staff members diligently working in silos, devoting their days to laboring in isolation from colleagues. Classroom doors remain tightly shut from the morning bell's welcoming of the new school day until the afternoon bell's signaling of the day's end. Even within a world of increased connectedness resulting from innovative digital tools and resources, the profession of teaching sometimes stands in stark contrast, remaining remarkably isolating for many educators.

Today's teachers must grapple with the realities of high-stakes accountability; in response, district leaders find themselves increasingly grasping for strategies to heighten their faculty members' efficacy in meeting the demands of the current educational landscape. In search of swift and sweeping solutions, administrators plan mandatory professional development experiences. They invest substantial amounts of money and time in interventions that may not result in lasting changes in educator practice or enhanced student engagement and achievement.

The frequently arbitrary execution of professional development strategies naturally results in interventions that lack overarching, clear purpose, thus failing to inspire faculty and staff members in the pursuit of educational excellence. Generic professional development experiences for teachers have historically been perceived as somewhat isolating and irrelevant.

More traditional models typically result in educators being subject to and reliant upon the itineraries and perspectives of outside "experts"—experts unfamiliar with the intricacies of the school culture or the most pressing needs of individual teachers. By their very nature, these sessions are often universally structured to address the needs of many participants. As a result, they tend to effectively support only a handful of attendees.

Recent professional development–related research highlights mixed results in terms of the efficacy of such strategies. For instance, a study involving four districts serving a predominantly low-income population of learners discovered that even with substantial financial investments in faculty professional development, teacher performance (according to teacher evaluations) and student learning (according to state assessments) experienced only minor impacts (TNTP, 2015).

In fact, the study uncovered that teacher evaluations remained the same, or even worsened, over the span of two to three years; simultaneously, these districts spent more than $18,000 of professional development funding per teacher on these endeavors. In spite of the outcomes of the research, the authors of this particular study refrained from recommending that districts rethink their investment in professional development. Instead, they recommended that school leaders redefine their processes of supporting teacher improvement, reassess current professional development programs, and reinvent strategies for supporting educators in their quest for teaching excellence.

Unfortunately, professional development opportunities do not always signify a pathway to increased professional learning and growth. Fullan (2007) asserts that external approaches to organizational advancement are seldom "powerful enough, specific enough, or sustained enough to alter the culture of the classroom and school" (p. 35).

In reality, research regarding professional development in the United States discovered that a majority of educators receive professional development in brief segments (fewer than eight hours per topic, typically in workshops after the school day has concluded). Interestingly, during the No Child Left Behind era, educators were more frequently exposed to short-term professional development approaches and encountered fewer ongoing professional development measures (Wei, Darling-Hammond, & Adamson, 2010).

Furthermore, some school settings present equity issues in relation to the effects of professional development upon student learning endeavors. For example, inadequate leadership, lack of resources, and counteracting district-level and schoolwide directives may all impact faculty members' access to effective professional development solutions (Buczynski & Hansen, 2010; Johnson & Fargo, 2010; Santagata, Kersting, Givvin, & Stigler, 2010).

THE REALITY OF ISOLATION WITHIN SCHOOL SETTINGS

The art of teaching represents an undeniably complex daily undertaking. Researchers estimate that throughout the course of one day at school, educators often make more than three thousand nontrivial decisions. Teachers must consistently assimilate their understanding of student cognition, their knowledge of the subject matter at hand, and various strategies for conveying their subject matter knowledge—all while integrating ever-changing digital tools and resources.

Even considering the complexity of educators' daily functioning, teaching continues to be viewed as a predominantly individualistic profession. Many decision-making endeavors are conducted in isolation, and collaboration among colleagues is sometimes lacking. Furthermore, when collaboration occurs, interaction is often limited to an interchange of day-to-day anecdotes or to sharing tips and tricks for enhancing lessons (Hargreaves & Daw, 1990).

Professional development opportunities typically involve advice from off-site "experts" through campus-based or district-level in-service workshops, many of which result from administrative directives. While implementation of these types of professional development experiences—whether optional or required—may be well intentioned, the long-lasting impacts of such trainings are often limited. Their "one size fits all" design and delivery hinder the potential for transformation, especially considering their detachment from daily classroom practices. Lacking immediate application, these training endeavors often fall short of impacting educators in any significant or lasting sense.

Teachers naturally struggle to apply instructional frameworks that are detached from the classroom experiences they encounter daily. Traditional group-based professional development endeavors place participants in a passive role by design, encouraging them to simply consume information rather than create new leaning experiences. Furthermore, such professional development experiences rarely offer educators the chance to collaborate with colleagues in implementing strategies presented through these trainings.

THE IMPORTANCE OF MEANINGFUL COLLABORATION

Impactful collaboration necessitates both equity and shared learning between colleagues. In order for professional development to produce meaningful, lasting change among teachers, it is important that those involved play a significant role in the process of reflection and growth. The most valuable professional development opportunities afford teachers an increasingly active role in their own learning. The perspectives of educators should be shared within the contexts of their own school and classroom environments, thus giving them to opportunity to journey together in developing as professionals within an authentic academic setting.

Over the years, numerous researchers have investigated the impacts of teachers' personal knowledge and its influence on their reasoning and decision-making processes (Elbaz, 1983; Clandinin, 1986; Connelly & Clandinin, 1988). Time and time again, researchers have discovered the inherent value of educators' experiential knowledge. Such studies emphasize teachers' propensity for choosing wise courses of action amid ever-changing, frequently unpredictable educational contexts.

Thus, the art of teaching is now conveyed in such terms as "personal practical knowledge" or a "moral, affective, and aesthetic way of knowing life's educational situations" (Connelly & Clandinin, 1988, p. 59). Such investigations of the abiding value of teacher knowledge impart educators' voices with heightened strength, especially within the spheres of academic research and professional development. This furthermore alludes to the complexity of each teacher's calling.

These findings, garnered from multiple sources of research, highlight important implications regarding professional development methods. More specifically, they speak to imperative of moving from strategies directed toward teachers in isolation; rather, innovative professional development endeavors provide educators with meaningful opportunities to participate in deeper modes of reflection, personally as well as alongside colleagues.

The professional development method known as collegial coaching serves to actively engage educators in reflecting upon their current, immediate professional practices. It offers participants the opportunity to become creators of their own pertinent knowledge and skills. Ultimately, coaching as a professional development model recognizes the magnitude of each teacher's individual needs and responsibilities within the realm of a classroom setting, while expanding learning for both the students and the professional.

Site-based experiences such as coaching for technology integration offer educators the opportunity to join with colleagues in collaborative growth. By their very nature, these personalized professional development endeavors allow teachers' unique skills and insights to be brought to light, giving them to chance to share in new ways with others. This type of professional development implicates a shift from isolated methods of training to shared, communal growth.

Collaborative experiences may be especially helpful as teachers face fears of the unknown while engaging in innovative learning experiences. Such fears may rise to the surface, for example, as more seasoned teachers contemplate the implementation of cutting-edge technologies. An educator may simply observe as a professional trainer uses digital tools and resources in an off-campus professional development workshop, but this does not imply that this same teacher will be able to readily return to the classroom and meaningfully reproduce the uses demonstrated during the workshop.

Any number of mishaps may occur during the implementation process. For example, an internet site that was easily accessible at home may be blocked by campus- or district-based filters, or an outdated app may not function properly during a lesson. Countless unknowns loom to prevent novice technology users from journeying beyond their comfort zones and engaging in new instructional experiences. Alternatively, when a collegial coach is available to scaffold the implementation process, fears of unknown technological difficulties seem to fade for many educators.

THE IMPERATIVE OF REFLECTION IN PROFESSIONAL DEVELOPMENT PRACTICES

Foundational concepts regarding reflection rest in Dewey's (1933) analysis of reflective reasoning. He viewed reflection as a vital means of facilitating educators' ability to develop effective courses of action with anticipated results in sight. Furthermore, he defined reflective cognition as the "active, persistent, and careful consideration of any belief or supposed form of knowledge in the light of the grounds that support it and the further conclusions to which it tends" (p. 9).

Dewey defined authentic reflection as that which shifts human behaviors from simple impulses into logical actions. While nonreflective instruction may feel mundane, programmed, and constrained, teachers who effectively use reflection move beyond a manifestation of professional behaviors shaped and mandated by others. Moreover, they distinguish issues, investigate ideas, contemplate innovative strategies, consider various opportunities, and create applicable educational experiences for the benefit of learners.

The incorporation of reflection in teaching strategies demonstrates tremendous promise for advancing professional practices; when this reflection takes place in collaboration with colleagues, the outcome frequently leads to more meaningful learning experiences.

Currently, the number of schools implementing methods of instructional coaching is growing at an astonishing rate. These nontraditional professional development strategies correlate closely with the importance of reflective practice. The tenets of application, teamwork, and deliberation comprise the groundwork of professional development involving authentic reflection. Additionally, these experiences recognize the distinctive and intricate methods of reasoning conveyed through professional action, as well as various approaches to transmitting experience and expertise from one educator to another.

A number of years ago, Knight (2006) recognized the needed shift in professional development methods, commenting that "coaching is becoming popular, in part, because many educational leaders recognize that the old form of professional development, built around traditional in-service sessions for teachers, simply doesn't affect student achievement" (p. 36). Consequently, the influence of teachers' connections with colleagues in a real-life classroom setting remains a key factor in designing professional growth experiences.

Reflective experiences focusing on educators' successes, failures, growth, and setbacks collectively enhance teaching practices. Likewise, constructive, nonevaluative feedback from a trusted colleague offers the potential to bring greater impact to these reflective experiences. Educators profit from opportunites to implement key teaching innovations "under good conditions and get help in the form of instruction, supervision, and feedback" (Siedentop & Tannehill, 2000, p. 3).

EXTENDING THE CONCEPT OF "LEARNING BY DOING"

A name often referenced within research focusing on reflective practice and pedagogical development is that of Donald Schön (1983; 1987). Expanding on the findings of Dewey, Schön extends the concept of learning by doing, recommending a pedagogical epistemology that places technical problem-solving procedures within the broader framework of reflective inquiry.

Schön maintains that professional development has conventionally placed too much prominence on scientific theories and overly clear-cut means of identifying solutions to issues. Thus, off-site, isolated professional development approaches often fail to fully equip teachers with the competencies necessary to effectively navigate the unanticipated and challenging incidences they will undoubtedly face in the real world, or what Schön (1983) labels the "swampy lowlands" (p. 3).

From Schön's viewpoint, "reflection-in-action" signifies the capacity to reflect prior to a situation in which obvious solutions and scientific models seem extraneous. "Reflection-on-action" involves reflecting upon the experience following its occurrence. Activities that require reflection before reaction when clear solution may not be evident (reflection-in-action), as well as those that require careful reflection following action (reflection-on-action), encompass necessary elements of meaningful professional development endeavors.

Collegial coaching empowers the coach and coachee to use both reflection-in-action and reflection-on-action as they reflect together on new strategies fresh on their minds, both in the midst of, as well as after, key teaching experiences. This type of coaching cultivates the art of reflection as a vital component of professional practice.

THE DAWN OF COACHING WITHIN EDUCATIONAL SETTINGS

Curiously, formal attempts to evaluate professional development endeavors within school settings began only in the last half of the twentieth century. Showers and Joyce (1996) provide a methodical overview of the evolution of professional development practices and, more specifically, the advent of formalized coaching programs.

Preliminary efforts to improve teacher education in the mid-1950s mainly targeted academic excellence and social fairness. Initial evaluations of teacher development strategies uncovered that a nonsubstantial number of participants—perhaps as little as 10 percent—successfully implemented the strategies offered within more traditional professional development endeavors.

Though well-examined, the instructional strategies and curriculum design methods demonstrated throughout such professional development formats unsuccessfully sought to bring about lasting impacts within teachers' daily professional practices. Subsequently, these training endeavors neglected to significantly impact the learning of students.

Eventually, educational researchers and leaders began to more consistently agree that traditional professional development endeavors seldom bring about meaningful change, regardless of the funds invested or the public support surrounding these movements. Guided by Vygotsky's (1978) perception of growth as a social process and Bandura's (1971) concepts of social learning, studies in the 1970s progressively recognized the social nature of educator learning. Thus, educational research throughout this decade underscored the possible advantages of collegial coaching with rising frequency.

More explicitly, Vygotsky's work points to the notion that dialogue among individuals offers a mechanism through which to create meaning. During such conversations, educators engage in reciprocal learning experiences, growing alongside one another. Similarly, in collegial coaching interactions, opportunities to collaborate inspire teachers to untangle and implement innovative professional strategies more successfully.

Moreover, Bandura's research provides key insights regarding the impact of collegial coaching as it pertains to social learning. Social learning focuses upon opportunities for individuals to learn vicariously from one another by observing each other's actions and identifying correlated outcomes. In this sense, collegial coaching underscores the transformative power of reciprocal learning.

By the early 1980s, researchers began to recognize that modifications to the organization of school environments and modes of professional development might support the transmission of knowledge from hypothetical theories to daily practice. Additionally, the notion of placing blame upon teachers for the shortcomings of traditional professional development endeavors seemed progressively more unjustified.

Interestingly, based on more than 150 interviews with educators from across the United States, Knight (2007) found that teachers rarely actively oppose change. More often, they oppose inadequately designed programs for change. Educators are inundated with what Fullan and Hargreaves (1996) refer to as "pressing immediacy," continually encountering more papers to grade, parents to contact, data to gather and evaluate, and lesson plans to create—not to mention classes to teach!

Many teachers' hesitancy to implement instructional innovation does not result from a lack of desire to incorporate new ideas or instructional tools; rather, they may face rational concerns that developing new strategies will consume a tremendous amount of time. For typically overburdened teachers, carving out extra time over the course of a day may seem unrealistic. Yet, when journeying alongside a collegial coach, the planning workload can be shared.

Joyce and Showers (1980) first introduced coaching models based on a wide-ranging review of literature overviewing the types of training most likely to bring about meaningful instructional transformation. The professional development mechanisms featured in their original research included modeling, practice, structured and open-ended feedback, the presentation of theory, and in-class support with knowledge and skill transmission. Joyce and Showers suggested that educators seeking to incorporate innovative methods within their professional repertoire would need ongoing technical support in their classroom contexts.

Their initial research comprised a formal investigation and subsequent verification of the premise that coaching after preliminary training ultimately results in a more successful transfer of concepts than training in seclusion (Showers, 1982, 1984). Early studies categorically show that educators who took part in coaching programs executed innovative teaching practices more regularly and applicably than colleagues who sought to improve their teaching practices alone. Collegial coaching participants exhibited increased recollection of novel methods and future applications of such strategies over prolonger timeframes (Baker & Showers, 1984).

AN EXPANDING FORM OF PROFESSIONAL GROWTH

Collegial coaching embodies a growing method of collaborative professional development within today's educational contexts. Through their research exploring the nature and impacts of collaborative professional development, Valencia and Killion (1988) describe collegial coaching as "the process where teams of teachers regularly observe one another and provide support, companionship, feedback, and assistance" (p. 170). Although this collaborative method of professional development began in K–12 school environments, even within postsecondary settings, the impact of collegial coaching programs expanded over the years.

Educators who engage in collegial coaching alongside a colleague with technology expertise show a nearly 90 percent execution rate (Hargreaves & Daw, 1990). Teachers participating in coaching experiences (a) implement new instructional strategies with improved frequency and obtain added skills, (b) integrate innovative approaches more appropriately, (c) employ these newfound strategies recurrently over time, and (d) share the thinking behind instructional strategies with learners.

Early theoretical investigations of collegial coaching depict a voluntary, nonevaluative framework built upon trust between colleagues. This approach serves to reciprocally benefit two teachers with similar professional experiences (Joyce & Showers, 1980). Initial research reveals that collegial coaching frequently requires teachers to engage in shared professional development activities, devising individually set goals for applying new knowledge to instructional practices. By the nature of this model, both educators concurrently participate in enhancing their teaching strategies.

Although collegial coaching began as a professional development framework involving equal partners, over the years, methods of coaching have developed to include expert coaching, reciprocal coaching, intradisciplinary coaching, and interdisciplinary coaching. This book distinctively concentrates on coaching relationships that exist between two equivalent partners—both of whom may be outstanding educators—in which the coach has greater technological expertise. In the present age of rapidly expanding digital innovation within educational settings and beyond, professional development targeting content-focused, pedagogically sound, results-based technology integration remains an area of tremendous need.

Collegial coaching is built, first and foremost, upon relationships. When this professional development framework is executed effectively, the coach fundamentally functions as a one-person support team for the coached colleague. The coached teacher receives individualized and continuing attention, and both the coach and coachee experience innovative ideas and viewpoints. This allows teachers within educational contexts to reimagine, restructure, and revitalize their professional practices in ways that revolutionize and enhance instructional strategies and learner achievement.

Within the following chapters, collegial coaching techniques will be investigated in greater depth, particularly in light of the distinctive aspects surrounding coaching for technology integration. Additionally, readers will encounter strategies for deciphering how to meet the specific needs of unique educators most effectively within various educational settings.

ESSENTIAL IDEAS TO REMEMBER

Collegial coaching programs have been praised as an essential professional development strategy for supporting teachers in facing the challenges of their calling as educators. The array of research in favor of this model highlights the effectiveness of coaching for improving teachers' professional learning experiences, eventually leading to enhanced student learning and success.

In this chapter and throughout the remainder of the book, readers will likely recognize an overarching theme: specifically, that no matter the structure of the collegial coaching program, the process must eventually serve "to build communities of teachers who continually engage in the study of their craft" (Showers, 1985, p. 43). Though sometimes taking on various forms, collegial coaching represents a valuable model for providing relevant and transformative professional development for educators.

REFERENCES

Baker, R. G., & Showers, B. (1984). *The effects of a coaching strategy on teachers' transfer of training to classroom practice: A six-month follow-up study*. New Orleans, LA: American Educational Research Association.
Bandura, A. J. (1971). *Social learning theory*. New York, NY: General Learning Press.
Buczynski, S., & Hansen, C. B. (2010). Impact of professional development on teacher practice: Uncovering connections. *Teaching and Teacher Education, 26*(3), 599–607.
Clandinin, J. (1986). *Classroom practice: Teacher images in action*. Lewes, Sussex, and Philadelphia: Falmer Press.
Connelly, M., & Clandinin, J. (1988). *Teachers as curriculum planners: Narratives of experience*. New York, NY: Teachers College Press.
Dewey, J. (1933). *How we think: A restatement of the relation of reflective thinking to the educative process*. Chicago, IL: D.C. Heath.
Elbaz, F. (1983). *Teacher thinking: A study of practical knowledge*. London, UK: Croom Helm.
Fullan, M. (2007). *The new meaning of educational change* (4th ed.). New York, NY: Teachers College Press, Columbia University.
Fullan, M., & Hargreaves, A. (1996). *What's worth fighting for in your school?* New York, NY: Teachers College Press.
Hargreaves, A., & Daw, R. (1990). Paths of professional development: Contrived congeniality, collaborative culture, and the case of peer coaching. *Teaching and Teacher Education, 6*, 227–41.
Johnson, C. C., & Fargo, J. D. (2010). Urban school reform enabled by transformative professional development: Impact on teacher change and student learning of science. *Urban Education, 45*(1), 4–29.
Joyce, B., & Showers, B. (1980). Improving inservice training: The messages of research. *Educational Leadership, 37*(5), 379–85.
Knight, J. (2006). Instructional coaching. *School Administrator, 63*(4), 36–40.
Knight, J. (2007). *Instructional coaching: A partnership approach to improving instruction*. Thousand Oaks, CA: Corwin Press.
Santagata, R., Kersting, N., Givvin, K. B., & Stigler, J. W. (2010). Problem implementation as a lever for change: An experimental study of the effects of a professional development program on students' mathematics learning. *Journal of Research on Educational Effectiveness, 4*(1), 1–24.
Schön, D. A. (1983). *The reflective practitioner: How professionals think in action*. New York, NY: Basic Books.
Schön, D. A. (1987). *Educating the reflective practitioner*. San Francisco, CA: Jossey-Bass.
Showers, B. (1982). *Transfer of training: The contribution of coaching*. Eugene, OR: Center for Educational Policy and Management.
Showers, B. (1984). *Peer coaching: Strategy for facilitating transfer of training*. Eugene, OR: Center for Educational Policy and Management.
Showers, B. (1985). Teachers coaching teachers. *Educational Leadership, 43*, 43–48.
Showers, B., & Joyce, B. (1996). The evolution of peer coaching. *Educational Leadership, 53*, 12-16.
Siedentop, D., & Tannehill, D. (2000). *Developing teaching skills in physical education* (4th ed.). Mountain View, CA: Mayfield.
TNTP. (2015). *The mirage: Confronting the hard truth about our quest for teacher development*. Brooklyn, NY: TNTP.
Valencia, S. W., & Killion, J. P. (1988). Overcoming obstacles to teacher change: Direction from school-based efforts. *Journal of Staff Development, 9*(2), 168–74.

Vygotsky, L. (1978). *Mind in society*. Cambridge, MA: Harvard University Press.
Wei, R. C., Darling-Hammond, L., & Adamson, F. (2010). *Professional development in the United States: Trends and challenges* (vol. 28). Dallas, TX: National Staff Development Council.

Chapter Two

Coaches to the Rescue in an Age of Rapid Response

"Teamwork is the ability to work together toward a common vision. The ability to direct individual accomplishments toward organizational objectives. It is the fuel that allows common people to attain uncommon results."—Andrew Carnegie

In today's increasingly digital world, teachers consistently encounter challenges not previously anticipated by past generations of educators. The lives of today's learners include an abundance of technological tools and resources, providing them unprecedented access to information on any imaginable subject. Consistent digital connectedness allows them to create and instantaneously distribute multimedia content to individuals across the globe.

Online social networking opportunities enable learners of the present age to interact with others from various part of the world, providing them an increasingly broader audience with which they can convey ideas, collaborate, and learn alongside. Beyond the borders of their school contexts, students enjoy virtually boundless autonomy to follow their passions. For countless learners of today, technical innovations represent immense, instant opportunities.

Chapter 2
THE POSSIBILITIES AND PITFALLS OF DIGITAL INNOVATION

Within this digitally dependent age, an undeniable challenge for educators and educational leaders involves leveraging today's technological advances to produce engaging, relevant, and memorable educational experiences for every learner. Such opportunities should reflect students' daily lives while priming them for upcoming academic, professional, and personal pursuits.

Rather than basing such learning experiences on more traditional instructional methods, a complete pedagogical paradigm shift is needed. In today's educational landscape, teachers face an ever-heightening demand for movement from teacher-centered to student-centered learning experiences. Digital tools and resources, when integrated effectively within classroom settings, empower educators to position learners as the focus, thus enabling students to guide the course of their own learning and providing enhanced flexibility and greater space for creativity.

A 2013 Pew Research Center survey focusing upon nearly twenty-five hundred Advanced Placement (AP) and National Writing Project (NWP) instructors demonstrates that teachers believe that digital tools and resources have advanced their instruction of middle school and high school students in numerous ways (Purcell, Heaps, Buchanan, & Friedrich, 2013). In fact, 92 percent of those surveyed indicate that the internet has been a "major impact" on their access of information and materials for instruction.

In this study, almost 70 percent of the AP teachers surveyed recognize that internet resources have substantially impacted their ability to work in partnership with fellow educators through communicating ideas, and approximately the same number indicate that online access has significantly affected their interactions with students' parents. Finally, 57 percent of those surveyed perceive that the internet has produced a considerable impact upon their communication with students.

Simultaneously, however, many educators believe that unfettered access to digital tools and resources brings a variety of new, unfamiliar issues to confront within school settings. In fact, 75 percent of the teachers surveyed feel that technological advances have imparted numerous extra demands upon their instructional practices. Specifically, they perceive that such innovations increase the scope of knowledge and skills in which they must demonstrate proficiency. Moreover, 41 percent of the educators surveyed indicate that increased access to new digital tools and resources necessitates additional work from them to teach effectively. Furthermore, clear generational disparities exist among educators in relation to their comfort levels with implementing digital tools and resources. Reflecting similar trends in the general adult population, variations in technological proficiency between more seasoned and newer teachers still exist. More explicitly, while 64 percent of educators under thirty-five years of age perceive themselves as being "very confident" in implementing innovative digital technologies, only 44 percent of those of fifty-five years of age or older hold similar confidence levels with regard to technology use.

Not unexpectedly, younger teachers often express a higher likelihood of supporting students in generating or sharing work via websites, blogs, or digital portfolios. Moreover, less veteran educators are more likely than their more experienced fellow teachers to plan for student participation in online discussions and to incorporate student collaboration using web-based tools such as Google Docs, Google Slides, and Google Sheets to cocreate and edit assignments. Furthermore, younger educators are increasingly prone to work in partnership with colleagues on developing ideas for technology implementation within instructional practices (22 percent of teachers under the age of thirty-five in comparison to 13 percent of educators over age fifty-five; Purcell, Heaps, Buchanan, & Friedrich, 2013).

For a number of years, most educators and parents have viewed digital tools and resources as an essential component of delivering a quality educational experience (Ertmer, 2005). Still, if this is the case, why do many teachers struggle to effectively incorporate technological innovations within their classroom settings in meaningful ways? Even for some educators who seem eager and willing to fully implement digital tools and resources into instructional practices, certain undeniable barriers prevent effective incorporation.

Faced with heightened directives for accountability, many of today's teachers grapple with allocating time in their increasingly packed schedules to research the latest technological innovations, let alone incorporate digital tools and resources within the curriculum. At most, some educators simply integrate technology as a means of checking this "to do" off the list, rather than strategically and intentionally implementing digital tools and resources to modify or redefine learning experiences for students. Encouragement and support in doing so is essential, more so now than ever before in the history of education.

Ertmer and colleagues (2003) discovered two categories of barriers to meaningful technology integration: namely, extrinsic (first order) and intrinsic (second order). Extrinsic barriers might involve limited resources, inadequate training, lack of technical support, and time constraints. Intrinsic barriers include teachers' attitudes, perceptions of technology integration, and confidence levels. Even in spite of the reality of such barriers, each may be successfully addressed through thoughtful collaboration and applicable learning experiences shared shoulder to shoulder with a fellow colleague.

HALLMARKS OF LEARNING IN THE DIGITAL AGE

As the expansion of technical innovation persists in today's educational landscapes, teachers must be increasingly prepared to foster and implement needed proficiencies for professionals in the digital age. For educators, simply possessing the ability to use technology is no longer enough.

Teachers in the digital age must expertly facilitate learning experiences in which students leverage technology to explore, discover, and display understanding. By incorporating authentic technical tools into learning experiences, teachers generate memorable encounters that inspire students to wrestle with real-life issues. Opportunities such as these prepare students to engage in future experiences, both as learners in the classroom and eventually as professionals in workplace settings.

VITAL KNOWLEDGE AND SKILLS FOR LEARNERS IN THE DIGITAL AGE

Empowered Learner

The International Society for Technology in Education (ISTE) provides a set of standards for evaluating essential skills and knowledge needed for students to engage in transformative learning with technology. Not surprisingly, learner empowerment ranks at the top of this list. More specifically, students of digital age should "leverage technology to take an active role in choosing, achieving, and demonstrating competency in their learning goals, informed by the learning sciences" (ISTE, 2016).

The value of fostering student-centered learning experiences is undeniable, and technological innovations have generated a countless variety of unique tools for enriching this process. According the ISTE (2016), today's students should have opportunities to develop personal learning goals, formulate strategies for using technology to accomplish these goals, and reflect upon their learning endeavors as a means of improving related learning outcomes.

Additionally, learners within current classroom settings should be supported in designing networks and tailoring their educational environments to further guide their learning processes. These network-building endeavors may involve online collaborations with other learners or experts in the field, such as through social media, videoconferencing opportunities, blogs involving reader engagement, and the like. They should use digital tools and resources to obtain feedback that informs and enhances their learning, and they should apply innovative technologies to exhibit their learning.

Furthermore, students should grasp the fundamentals of technology-related knowledge and skills, expressing their proficiency through selecting, using, and troubleshooting appropriate technologies, as well as applying their knowledge and skills toward discovering emerging technological tools and resources.

Digital Citizen

According to ISTE, the second set of skills essential for creating learning opportunities in the current age centers on digital citizenship. Today's learners should "recognize the rights, responsibilities and opportunities of living, learning, and working in an interconnected digital world, and they act in ways that are safe, legal and ethical" (ISTE, 2016). More specifically, this entails fostering and maintaining their digital identity and online reputation, remaining cognizant of the permanent implications of their digitally based activities within society.

Students should also participate in helpful, legal, safe, and ethical actions when using digital tools and resources, including their social networking activities. Additionally, they should be well versed regarding the rights and responsibilities of using and distributing intellectual property. Furthermore, students should maintain their personal data in ways that sustain their digital safety and privacy, and they should be cognizant of technologies designed to track their online activities.

Those responsible for guiding younger generations—including today's educators—hold the potential to help build outstanding digital citizens of future years. But unless teachers are armed with adequate knowledge and real-world experience with displaying effective digital citizenship in their personal and professional lives, how will they be able to convey these skills to others? To what degree might support from a knowledgeable teammate advance this endeavor?

Knowledge Constructor

The third set of ISTE (2016) standards involves students' ability to "critically curate a variety of resources using digital tools to construct knowledge, produce creative artifacts and make meaningful learning experiences for themselves and others." Along these lines, students should plan and execute efficacious research methods to identify information that aligns with their academic and creative endeavors. They should effectively appraise the validity and reliability of data, media, and other resources. Furthermore, they should apply a variety of strategies to curate collections of research and artifacts. They should also create new learning experiences through strategically exploring real-life issues, developing hypotheses, and seeking applicable solutions.

In a world in which information sources—whether reliable and beneficial or misleading and insufficient—may be easily located through the click of a mouse or the tap of a screen, the importance of acquiring research and information fluency cannot be overstated. Today's learners are regularly inundated with too much instead of too little information. Therefore, the greatest task comes in interpreting how to use the information at hand most effectively, as well as in determining which data to reject.

Without direction in acquiring these skills, students may struggle to effectively leverage resources and make use of the available information. Consequently, now more than ever, today's educators must acquaint themselves with the most useful means of discovering, organizing, and assessing online sources of information so that they can effortlessly communicate these crucial proficiencies to their students.

Innovative Designer

In addition to the previously considered standards, the capacity to engage in creative design processes ranks among the most imperative of the digital age. As noted by ISTE (2016), students should be able to apply a "variety of technologies within a design process to identify and solve problems by creating new, useful, or imaginative solutions." They should recognize and employ a strategic design process for formulating ideas, testing hypotheses, and producing creative artifacts of learning or solving real-world issues. They should identify and use digital tools and resources to prepare and oversee design processes that take potential limitations and risks into account. Additionally, they should cultivate, assess, and enhance models as components of the design process. Finally, students should display acceptance of uncertainty, persistence, and the ability to work with problems that are not easily answered.

Yet, during a time in which many educators daily encounter schedules packed to capacity as well as ever more scripted curricular frameworks, how regularly are they given the chance to innovate within their own professional lives? How often are they supported in inventing new strategies or tools to solve issues within their own classroom contexts?

Many teachers find themselves filling each day with addressing the required curriculum and instructing students in preparation for standardized assessments; sometimes, limited time remains for truly imaginative, inventive pursuits. In such cases, it is especially challenging to visualize how educators might employ digital tools in classroom contexts to ignite students' imaginations and innovative capabilities.

Computational Thinker

The next standard highlighted by ISTE involves the ability to think computationally. More specifically, students should "use a variety of technologies within a design process to identify and solve problems by creating new, useful, or imaginative solutions" (ISTE, 2016). For example, they should generate problem definitions applicable to technology-assisted techniques, such as the analysis of data and theoretical models in investigating and identifying solutions. They should collect pertinent data, applying digital tools to evaluate the data and ultimately representing their findings through various means to enable effective problem-solving and decision-making endeavors.

Furthermore, students should simplify problems into various elements, isolating key components and developing expressive models to better comprehend intricate systems. They should understand automation processes and use algorithms to develop sequential steps to design and assess automated results.

The advantages of supporting students in fostering skills in critical thinking, problem solving, and decision making cannot be overstressed. In today's world, digital tools and resources, when executed successfully, play a significant part in accelerating the development of these standards. In fact, more and more professional fields will require that their incoming hires be proficient at implementing such skills through digital applications.

Learners enthusiastically await chances to apply various technologies in their endeavors to reason, solve problems, and articulate decisions. Outside of the school day, many students spend significant portions of time doing this through digital games and programs intended to challenge the mind and develop computational processes. Yet, when similar learning experiences with technology are unavailable within classroom contexts, students unsurprisingly find it more difficult to stay consistently engaged over the course of the school day.

There sometimes appears to be a gulf between how learners are expected to participate at school, how they challenge their minds outside of the school day, and what they might be required to do upon entering professional contexts. What could happen if increasing numbers of teachers were more comfortable with effectively implementing engaging, interactive digital tools and resources within their lessons? How might this serve to generate innovative connections between classroom experiences, the activities and passions students engage in on their own, and the knowledge and skills they will need to function effectively in the future?

Creative Communicator

Creative communication represents another key ISTE standard for students in the digital age. Students in today's world should "communicate clearly and express themselves creatively for a variety of purposes using the platforms, tools, styles, formats and digital media appropriate to their goals" (ISTE, 2016). For example, students should select suitable digital tools and resources for achieving stated objectives. They should generate original artifacts of learning or repurpose digital resources into novel constructs. Additionally, they should convey intricate ideas with clarity and effectiveness. Finally, they should also create and share content that adapts the message and the mode of communication for the audience at hand.

With each passing day, cutting-edge digital tools and resources emerge for extending humankind's capacity to communicate with others, whether a coworker in the classroom next door or an acquaintance halfway around the world. Whereas collaboration was once restricted to the times and locations in which participants could be present physically, people can now collaborate at all hours of each day and from any location, irrespective of geographic locales and time zones.

Webster-Smith, Albritton, and Kohler-Evans (2012) observed, "People in organizations unknowingly cry out for meaningful conversations that are positive, fruitful, and constructive. The significance of meaningful conversations is especially critical in schools where administrators and teachers are either working in isolation or at cross-purposes" (p. xii). Just as educational professionals "cry out" for opportunities to meaningfully communicate and work in partnership with other committed teachers, today's learners seek to create points of connectedness with each another and to work collaboratively in a variety of learning ventures.

Teachers and students of today encounter a progressively fast-paced world in which many individuals find themselves gravitating toward the path of least resistance, obliged to consistently achieve the maximum amount of work within the minimum amount of time. Such endeavors often involve a sense of remoteness, requiring disconnection from others.

Although heightened use of digital tools and resources is sometimes linked to an increased sense of isolation, digital innovation can also provide new means of improving communication and collaboration among educators and learners. Innovative technological tools and resources empower teachers and students to cooperate and create with contemporaries and experts, both inside of and beyond the confines of school contexts.

Global Collaborator

ISTE's (2016) final standard states that students should "use digital tools to broaden their perspectives and enrich their learning by collaborating with others and working effectively in teams locally and globally." Students should use digital tools to connect with others of various experiences and traditions, communicating with them in ways that expand reciprocal learning experiences. They should employ collaborative digital tools and resources to engage with others in investigating issues from diverse viewpoints. They should also productively contribute to collaborative work, taking on a variety of responsibilities to achieve common goals.

Recently, in fact, educational institutions across the globe faced a systemic transition to distance learning during the worldwide COVID-19 pandemic. In light of the need for teachers and students to pivot from in-person to remote instructional settings with minimal time for planning, there exists a pressing demand for coaching practices that empower teachers to deliver effective instruction in a variety of environments.

The Coaching CPR Method outlined in this book not only addresses the growth of teachers within face-to-face learning environments, but it also focuses upon the vitality of coaching that prepares teachers to seamlessly transition between instructional delivery modes. The remainder of the book will address the ways in which the Coaching CPR Method can be applied to both in-person and distance-learning environments, thus preparing educators to effectively navigate an ever-changing educational landscape.

As technical knowledge and skills such as those previously highlighted become progressively more sought after in professional contexts, neglecting to prepare today's learners for this reality is a tremendous disservice to them. The thought of hindering a student's capacity to succeed later in life grieves the heart of any passionate educator.

No devoted educator would intentionally relinquish their potential to provide motivating learning experiences, nor would they support the thought of graduating students without preparation for the future. For teachers, schools, and districts who desire more for their learners, collegial coaching holds the potential to expand educators' abilities to leverage instructional technology like never before.

ESSENTIAL IDEAS TO REMEMBER

Today's educators encounter many new challenges not previously encountered by professionals in the field. Faced with snowballing demands for accountability, many teachers struggle to devote time within their packed schedules to research cutting-edge digital tools and resources, let alone identify strategies for meaningfully incorporating them into the required curriculum. Encouragement and support in doing so is now more essential than ever before.

Opportunities to spark profound change through collegial coaching exist within educational environments everywhere. School settings abound with seasoned educators devoted to meeting their students' needs through relevant, engaging, and student-centered lessons and units. Such teachers eagerly desire to successfully implement instructional technology within their curriculum. The issue does not involve lacking the "want to"; rather, they sometimes simply lack the "how to." This is where the advantages of collegial coaching, and specifically the Coaching CPR Method, come into play.

REFERENCES

Ertmer, P. A. (2005). Teacher pedagogical beliefs: The final frontier in our quest for technology integration? *Educational Technology Research and Development*, *53*(4), 25–39.

Ertmer, P. A., Conklin, D., Lewandowski, J., Osika, E., Selo, M., & Wignall, E. (2003). Increasing preservice teachers' capacity for technology integration through the use of electronic models. *Teacher Education Quarterly*, 95–112.

International Society for Technology in Education (2016). *Standards•S*. Retrieved from https://www.iste.org/standards/for-students

Purcell, K., Heaps, A., Buchanan, J., & Friedrich, L. (2013). *How teachers are using technology at home and in their classrooms*. Retrieved from http://www.pewinternet. org/2013/02/28/how-teachers-are-using-technology-at-home-and-in-their-classrooms/

Webster-Smith, A., Albritton, S., & Kohler-Evans, P. (2012). *Meaningful conversations: The way to comprehensive and transformative school improvement*. Lanham, MD: Rowman & Littlefield Education.

Chapter Three

Deploying the Coaching CPR Model

> "The way a team plays as a whole determines its success. You may have the greatest bunch of individual stars in the world, but if they don't play together, the club won't be worth a dime." —Babe Ruth

Few individuals would deny the notion that digital innovation is transforming nearly every facet of daily existence. Undoubtedly, an ever-surging deluge of technological innovation is altering the way humankind views and interacts in today's world. Facing a perpetual state of flux that now seems status quo, few contexts are more greatly impacted than the realms of educational settings.

Today's teachers must confront the responsibility of preparing students for success in the years to come, even as unpredictable as those years might seem. Educators must instruct their students in legacy content as well as strategies for harnessing digital tools in critical thinking, communication, collaboration, and creative endeavors as they engage with the world around them. Unfortunately, many educators (even seasoned teachers) feel uncomfortable at the thought of innovatively integrating technology into learning pursuits.

Previous findings of Wilson, Alaniz, and colleagues demonstrate that collegial coaching for technology integration holds the power to effectively help teachers in conquering such fears and inhibitions (Wilson, Brupbacher, Simpson, & Alaniz, 2013; Alaniz & Wilson, 2015). Through this framework, technology-related professional development is accomplished via a coaching relationship that is individualized, targeted, and directly applicable to everyday classroom experiences.

As a result, teachers gain self-confidence and novel pedagogical strategies with the incorporation of coaching for technology integration, thus elevating the content knowledge for learners. Current research focuses specifically upon the process of augmenting collegial coaching for technology integration through the assimilation of the Technological Pedagogical Content Knowledge (TPCK) framework (Mishra, 2008), which later became TPACK framework (Koehler & Mishra, 2009), while also integrating Coaching for Technology Integration framework (Alaniz & Wilson, 2015).

While the TPACK framework focuses on active construction in teachers' professional practices (Herring, Koehler & Mishra, 2016), the Coaching CPR Method focuses on coaching the teacher to teach in a more student-centered approach, using technology as a tool to deliver and transform learning experiences. This model involves students' authentic engagement in real world inquiry that is active, constructive, and collaborative, while exhibiting their learning through the application of content specific technology tools (Howland, Jonassen, & Marra, 2012).

TEACHERS AND STUDENTS AS COCREATORS OF LEARNING

In educational environments, the promise of digital integration is vast. It holds the potential to advance learning opportunities for students around the world. When executed efficaciously, educational technology often enhances the scope and impact of skillful teaching (Lei & Zhao, 2007). It provides teachers with groundbreaking tools for reimagining the transfer of key concepts, thereby inspiring students to become cocreators of their own learning endeavors. The issue resides in the fact that technology incorporation fluctuates depending on the content area at hand and the developmental levels involved in the learning.

In the face of escalating demands for accountability, countless teachers lack the time to research innovative means of incorporating digital tools and resources into their instructional strategies (McCrary & Mazur, 2010). Integrating required standards and assessments with technology-rich learning experiences is often difficult for teachers, requiring more time than they can feasibly spare. Educators must make use of strategies for working cooperatively to accomplish such planning, instructional, and assessment learning goals with excellence

(Kopcha, 2010). Recognizing this need, many districts hire content specialists (or content coaches) while also separately employing instructional technologists. From nearly seventy case studies of instructional technology coaches working individually with teachers across numerous classroom contexts, evidence confirms the value of coaches from similar content area backgrounds in strengthening teachers' ability to integrate solid pedagogical and technological practices (Alaniz & Wilson, 2015).

In traditional professional development contexts, each attendee simply represents one audience member among sometimes countless other participants. Workshops such as this typically highlight a broad spectrum of subjects, each of which may or may not relate to the day-to-day experiences of educators and their students. The topics covered can easily fall short of tackling educators' most urgent concerns in relation to their priorities as teachers and goals for addressing students' academic needs (Knight, 2007).

Teachers are responsible for reflectively and expertly differentiating learning opportunities for their students. Nonetheless, the professional development experiences offered to educators are rarely tailored to address their individual instructional needs. Teachers, much like their students, appreciate learning experiences that provide them with immediately applicable concepts presented in engaging ways. For educators, as for the learners within their classrooms, scaffolding new teaching tools and strategies within a framework of application is crucial for bringing about impactful learning opportunities.

In the Coaching CPR Method, coaches are taught to digitally innovate, while being content specific, pedagogically sound, and focused on results. Instructional activities are targeted so that they support and engage a combination of learning tasks involving digital tools to learn *with*, rather than *from*. Effective teachers exhibit knowledge of the content as well as knowledge of pedagogy and technology, and effective coaches must be able to transition educators from simply using technology to transforming the learning as a result of technology use.

RESEARCHING COLLEGIAL COACHING IN ACTION

In 2014, I began working with my mentor, Dr. Dawn Wilson, to guide graduate students' coaching for technology integration in public and private schools across the city of Houston and beyond. These coaching

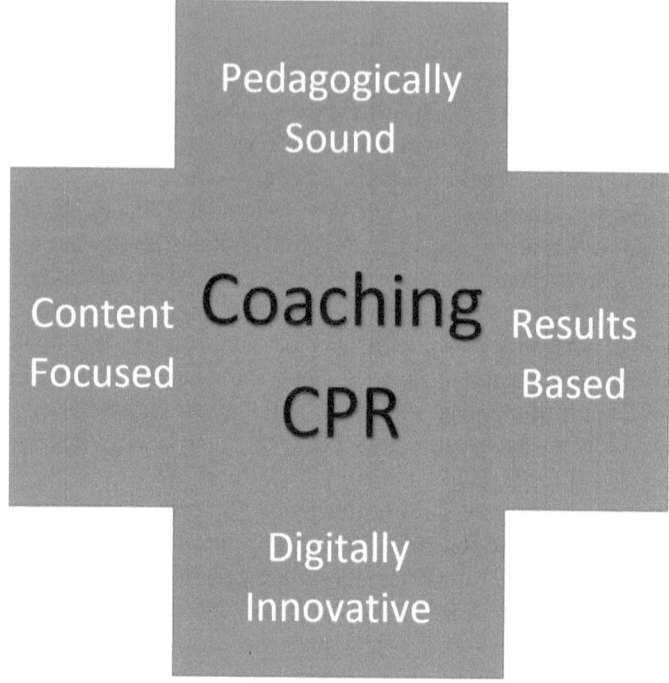

Figure 3.1. Coaching CPR Method

experiences comprised an integral component of a capstone course for students completing a Master of Education in Curriculum and Instruction with a specialization in Instructional Technology at Houston Baptist University. Due to the online expansion of the program, teachers across the United States also eventually participated in this research.

The program extended the graduate student coaches' background knowledge and skills with regard to technology integration, highlighted principles for successful coaching, and provided structure and continuing support throughout coaching processes. Because the coaching element of the capstone course required each student to pursue additional learning endeavors in preparation to address the most pressing needs of the colleagues they coached, the program stressed independent learning and knowledge of a wide range of digitals tools and applications. Throughout the coaching process, the graduate student coaches conferenced with their professor regularly in order to share coaching successes as well as to collaboratively brainstorm possible solutions to issues that arose.

During the semester-long coaching experience, the coaches and their coachees maintained journals articulating their observations regarding the coaching experience. At the conclusion of the coaching process, the coached teachers filled out a questionnaire assessing their experience. This questionnaire provided them the opportunity to appraise their coaches and their experience as coachees. It also gave them the chance to make suggestions for improvement of the coaching process as a whole.

Each coach, most of whom were also teachers in early childhood through high school settings, worked with three faculty members (coachees) on their home campus to support them in overcoming some of their recognized technology difficulties. Coaches devoted approximately fifteen hours to meeting with each coachee over the course of a semester, during which time they devised ideas for technology incorporation, formulated a plan, and implemented the collaboratively developed strategies. Coachees aimed to implement at least three novel technological tools with their students, with at least one application involving student-centered use.

As the coaches met with their coachees, they pursued a five-step process to support them in facilitating technology integration coaching. Over time, this process proved to be highly advantageous for teachers, whether digital natives (those with little technology experience) or those simply seeking to enhance their technology integration effectiveness. These five steps, which are outlined in the previous work of Alaniz and Wilson (2015), include: (1) establishing the need, (2) creating the partnership, (3) brainstorming and targeting integration projects, (4) assessing the outcomes, and (5) reflecting. As each new project was tackled, the coach circled back to steps 3 through 5 in order to solidify their coachees' self-confidence and effectiveness while also building student enthusiasm, engagement, and achievement.

The methods presented throughout this book have been integrated within school settings for several years with tremendous success, offering novice users of technology greater confidence in applying digital tools and resources to their own planning and instruction. In essence, these techniques provide a direct, clear-cut outline for coaches and teachers seeking to augment the efficacy and quality of technology integration within the contexts in which they serve.

It goes without saying that a one-size-fits-all methodology for collegial coaching for technology integration will almost certainly fall short of meeting the needs of any one educational environment. Thus, the five-step framework described in this book, previously outlined in Alaniz and Wilson's (2015) guidebook for collegial coaching, was created with the purpose of providing a basic roadmap to implementing a collegial coaching program among educators.

This method provides for flexibility and personalization. The speed at which participants travel through this journey, as well as the detours and rest stops they take along the way, will almost surely—and of necessity—vary from school to school and district to district. Most significantly, coaches and coached teachers should be given the necessary time and encouragement to appreciate the journey, contemplate their travels, and keep in mind that the process is often more important than the product.

CRITICAL COMPONENTS OF THE COACHING CPR METHOD

The central ideas for the collegial coaching process include what is known about adult learning theory, or andragogy, and project-based learning. First identified by Knowles in the 1970s, adult learning theory emphasizes six assumptions that focus upon how adults prefer to acquire new learning. These assumptions emphasize collaborative, problem-centered approaches that highlight equality between teachers and students. The following comprise the six principles of adult learning theory:

- Adults are internally motivated and self-directed.
- Adults bring life experiences and knowledge to learning experiences.
- Adults are goal oriented.
- Adults are relevancy oriented.
- Adults are practical.
- Adult learners like to be respected.

In the Coaching CPR Method, adults in the teaching profession will clearly be asked to learn new concepts. Very often, the concepts to be addressed have been averted over time, often because the coachee identifies them as either impractical or too difficult. Yet as specifics regarding this model unfold throughout this chapter and the remainder of the book, the strategies involved and rationales for its success should become increasingly evident.

In addition to principles of andragogy, the incorporation of project-based learning is also embedded within foundational aspects of the model. Project-based learning merges both intellectual and social constructivist theories from Jean Piaget and Lev Vygotsky by presenting authentic issues to solve in a collaborative approach through discussion, group processing, and reflection.

Though teachers are often urged to integrate project-based learning into their instructional design, educators themselves are rarely trained using this methodology. The advantages of project-based learning include heightened motivation, increased critical thinking, practice with problem solving, and the capacity to transfer knowledge and skills to new situations. Coached teachers find that using technology in many cases includes a transformation from teacher-centered to student-centered instructional practices. These benefits, among others, have been noted by educators participating in case studies of coaching for technology integration (Alaniz & Wilson, 2015).

A REAL-LIFE SOLUTION TO A REAL-LIFE PROBLEM

The model outlined in this book was born from an amalgamation of real-life classroom experiences, originating with students at the author's university. As described earlier, as a component of a graduate capstone project focusing on coaching for technology integration, students with technology expertise were each required to coach three teachers on their respective school campuses.

One of the coaches involved in the project—who also served as an instructional specialist at the time—chose to coach three seasoned educators who had previously avoided technology integration, each citing various reasons. Pam, the coach, discussed that these teachers demonstrated in the coaching process that "people want to learn, and it is less threatening to work with someone else instead of in isolation." She also remarked that the teachers she coached finally discovered a sense of freedom to "confess their areas of weakness so that those targeted areas could be addressed in a private setting with customized support" (Alaniz & Wilson, 2015, p. 37).

As this coaching model has steadily been refined over a number of years, five steps have proven imperative to the attainment of effective technology integration. As Pam remarked, "Coaching is nothing new to my district. We have been on the coaching bandwagon for many years, but this is the first time that coaching from the instructional technology perspective has been implemented." Moreover, she stressed, "Now that we are on the verge of a technology implementation breakthrough, the timing of the internship was perfect! This type of professional development is more effective because it's not a one-shot, drive-by, 'wham-bam' done" (Alaniz & Wilson, 2015, p. 38).

The Coaching CPR Model for technology integration is cyclical by nature, consisting of phases that intuitively interconnect with one another to form a complete, unified whole. Although these steps are described in progressive order in the following pages, coaches and coachees must remember that coaching participants can—and even *should*—revisit preceding phases at any time during the process as needed.

These steps are not intended to be checked off a to-do list upon completion. In fact, considering the intricate nature of interactions among individuals within organizations, there is not a cut-and-dried method of completing any one of the steps. Instead, progress within each of the phases and transitions back and forth between them should be thoughtfully reflected upon at various intervals along the way. The overview provided here aligns with the introduction of these phases first shared in the work of Alaniz and Wilson (2015) entitled *Naturalizing Digital Immigrants: The Power of Collegial Coaching for Technology Integration*.

THE FIVE PHASES OF THE COLLEGIAL COACHING MODEL FOR TECHNOLOGY INTEGRATION

Phase 1: Establish the Need

Before beginning any new journey, travelers should of course identify the purpose, or the "why," prompting them to embark upon their travels. Why should this journey commence? Are there personal reasons, professional reasons, or both? Will these travels bring about adventure, education and discovery, a break from daily routines, or some amalgamation of those reasons?

Much like the process of planning a tangible journey in life, effective organizational programs also find their basis in the authentic needs

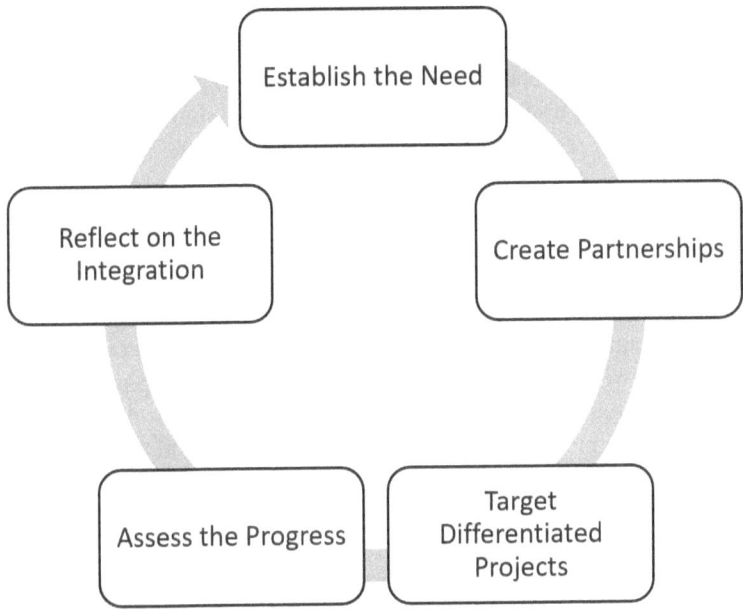

Figure 3.2. Coaching CPR Cycle

of stakeholders, or the "why." School administrators must first confer with potential audience members: namely, teachers on the front lines of student service. If collegial coaching is to prove useful within educational contexts, it should be intended to meet a definitive need within the school setting and for the prospective participants.

However, a substantial chasm may exist between the perceived needs of community members and the actual needs within the community, both in magnitude and type of support. Furthermore, it should be clear within that context that collegial coaching is the suitable response to addressing technology integration gaps. If a clear need does not exist, school leadership will likely face teachers apathetic to collegial coaching or possibly even averse to participation.

Prior to the commencement of the coaching process, school administrators must seek to understand what those involved might desire. If the coaching process will be introduced through a committee comprising school leadership, teachers, or both, it will be imperative to coordinate a comprehensive discussion determining the time frame, participants and their responsibilities, and other required resources.

Alternatively, school administrators might incorporate plans to directly gather the teachers' feedback. Online surveys or questionnaires shared via e-mail might provide a time-effective, simple means of collecting insights regarding individual faculty members' needs, desires, and willingness to take part in coaching endeavors. School leaders must remember that coaching is not intended only for educators without experience in technology implementation; it may also support seasoned teachers needing to fine-tune their knowledge and skills.

School administrators must also determine whether participation will be voluntary or mandatory. Furthermore, they must decide whether participants will be allowed to choose their own coaching partners or if partnerships will be selected for them. These significant decisions will likely render quite an impact upon teachers' enthusiasm toward participating in the coaching process.

Just as notably, those endeavoring to introduce a collegial coaching program must assess whether the school leadership team is unified in seeking enhanced technology integration within the educational setting. Is this a mutual goal among only some members of the administration and faculty, or is this an endeavor that each school leader earnestly wants?

School administrators should be prepared to actively communicate why enhanced technology integration is key. For example, teachers may be wondering whether this is simply a tactic to encourage integration of a variety of tools or if it is valuable because technology incorporation involves a pedagogical shift along with a focus on heightened student engagement and achievement. They must decide whether the school community is receptive to innovation or if there are some among the leadership and faculty teams that outspokenly (and even boisterously) resist such change.

Once reluctant teachers witness how increased technological proficiency enhances confidence, enthusiasm, and personal productivity, those less predisposed to the idea will possibly have a change of heart. Moreover, when coaching partnerships concentrate on tackling predetermined outcomes together or endeavor to accomplish a certain number of student-centered projects per semester, the coaching effort will gradually produce ripple effects over time. As faculty members who have greatly benefited from the collegial coaching process share about their successes with colleagues, interest and enthusiasm will likely be sparked in the minds of those who were initially resistant.

In the previously mentioned case studies involving collegial coaching for technology integration, coaches planned to individually meet with coachees for an initial diagnostic conference. During these interviews, the coaches supported the coached teachers in discussing their fears, qualms, uncertainties, and primary goals.

As previously mentioned, one objective for the coaches in the program involved guiding each of their three coached teachers through the process of incorporating at least three innovative digital tools and resources. Understandably, when provided the chance to self-identify and self-report targeted areas of growth, coachees were more personally driven to bring these projects to fruition.

Coaches in the case studies received the opportunity to serve on campuses across the city of Houston and beyond with the approval of school administrators, and coachees typically volunteered to take part in this endeavor. At times, however, school leadership selected faculty members in need of additional support with technology implementation, so that coaching processes might enhance their development in this area.

The chance to collaborate with a fellow colleague ranked among the primary factors participants attributed to the success of the coaching process. In collaboratively journeying together, they highlighted these previously mentioned principles of adult learning theory:

- Adults are internally motivated and self-directed.
- Adults bring life experiences and knowledge to learning experiences.

In the words of collegial coach Pam, it is incredibly important for the coach to "set the tone for the relationship." Furthermore, there should be "respect, and the coach must listen to and understand the teacher's goals, ideas, worries, concerns, hopes, and dreams" (Alaniz & Wilson, 2015, p. 42). Unsurprisingly, finding opportunities to build upon the coachees' strengths rather than concentrating on their shortcomings also provides more positive, meaningful results.

Phase 2: Create Partnerships

The process of thoughtfully selecting partnerships within collegial coaching programs cannot be overstated. Successfully pairing coaches and coached teachers requires careful planning and consideration. Indeed, collaborative relationships often constitute a practical means of enriching an organization's success, especially when they are rooted in meaningful communication and partnership. However, creating advantageous groups is not always as straightforward as this process might seem.

Collaborative partnerships gone sour might lead to aggravation, resentment, and loss of time, as well as depletion of community morale. A famous line from the movie *The Godfather* is Don Corleone's mantra, "It's business, not personal." Yet this belief does not typically hold true in collaborative partnerships, even in the professional context of a school setting. Because a variety of personalities come into play in the coaching process, partnerships will unquestionably involve both professional and personal dynamics.

Therefore, as partnerships are formed, time and careful thought must be devoted to the willingness and abilities of coaches and coachees to collaborate and communicate effectively with each other. When navigating human relationships, it is impossible to guarantee that the situation will consistently remain conflict free, no matter how well the pairs are matched. Most significantly, each partner should be prepared to thoughtfully deal with and learn as a result of conflicts as they occur.

Throughout the coaching process, coaches must remain mindful of the fact that theirs is a nonevaluative, partner-based role. Coaches should refrain from controlling the situation, instead listening as the coachees shares their needs. Each partner must retain a willingness to collaborate and a flexible demeanor through the process of collaboratively planning integration pieces. Partnerships should stay focused on creating and adhering to an action plan for accomplishing set goals.

Obviously, reciprocal respect is a critical aspect of successful coaching relationships. Participants will likely find it less challenging to communicate openly with a coach who is a peer than with a supervisor. In addition, when coaches and coachees find that they face similar issues within their professional contexts, encouraging professional networks often instinctively emerge. In collegial coaching programs, a significant piece of the reflective process involves self-identification of professional and personal goals that align with one's values (Bland, Taylor, Shollen, Weber-Main, & Mulcahy, 2009).

Apart from personality concerns, the design of partnerships also entails more technical considerations. When feasible, coaches should be matched with colleagues who teach similar content, thus heightening the probability that the will be able to effectively guide their coachees through curriculum-centric endeavors.

In early childhood and elementary settings, content-specific partnerships are naturally not difficult to establish, as most primary educators instruct in multiple, if not all, subject areas. In these cases, pairs may be selected within grade-level teams if at all possible, thus enabling coaches to assist with projects spanning numerous content areas within a single grade level.

In secondary contexts, the subject area may in some cases influence the most appropriate technological tools. In higher-level settings, fitting digital tools and resources often vary greatly between content areas. For example, appropriate technologies within a high school calculus course might differ from those in an English or American history course.

Furthermore, Fibkins (2011) proposes that school leaders take on an active role in coaching programs. They might possibly even consider forming mentoring teams composed of teacher leaders, curriculum coordinators, department chairs, assistant principals, principals, and/or district leaders. In time, these colleagues will have the capacity to train others to serve as mentors within the school community. Such teams might meet occasionally to support one other in expanding the coaching process.

In the previously mentioned case studies regarding collegial coaching, the initial interview offered coaches important understandings regarding content to be focused upon within the coachees' curricular guidelines. These insights provided a foundation from which the coaches and coachees brainstormed for instructional strategies and tools that might be employed to teach or assess content. Lindsay, one of the coaches involved in the case studies, discovered that in meeting with her coachees, "we started with what they did in the past, and then talked about how we could tweak their already great lesson or unit to include technology to either deliver content or allow students to demonstrate their learning" (Alaniz & Wilson, 2015, p. 46).

Fellow coach Pam commented, "It was important to frame our conversations with, 'We are learning together!'" Knight (2011) described the tremendous value in reciprocity. He defines reciprocity as the idea that every learning interaction provides a chance for everyone to learn. In other words, "When one teaches, two learn" (Alaniz & Wilson, 2015, p. 46).

As coached teachers become more fully trained and receive new opportunities to develop self-confidence and skill in technology integration as well as in the art of coaching itself, the coaching circle begins to expand. These coached teachers will soon acquire the capacity to coach others, thus extending the cycle. Ultimately, this will hopefully lead to a schoolwide coaching program through which every member of the school faculty receives the opportunity to serve as a learner and as a learner.

Phase 3: Target Differentiated Technology Projects

After partnerships have been established, coaches and coachees should be ready to focus their attention on the goals or projects discussed within their initial meeting. This phase relates to the following adult learning theory principles:

- Adults are goal oriented.
- Adults are relevancy oriented.
- Adults are practical.

Because adults most effectively learn in situations that provide the chance to address a set goal or goals, well-specified projects should be established early in the coaching process. In doing so, the coaches and coached teachers will be more prepared to focus upon identified targets, rather than possibly wasting time and facing plummeting motivation by proceeding without direction. Moreover, adults desire to work toward achieving goals that seem applicable to their professional and personal needs; thus, the projects should be directly applicable to objectives they have set for themselves and for their students.

Finally, because adults most effectively learn in circumstances they recognize as practical, objectives for achieving predetermined projects must be reasonable. Before beginning any new projects, coaches and coachees should think through questions such as the following:

- Can this project be accomplished within the intended amount of time?

- If not, can this project be broken into smaller, more manageable pieces?
- Upon the project's completion, can it reasonably be integrated into the coached teacher's professional activities?

When beginning the coaching process with a teacher inexperienced in technology integration, coaches should focus first on goals associated with personal productivity. For instance, the coach could consider types of teacher-centered technology use that might support the coachee in simplifying day-to-day activities, such as digital file organization, presentation design, and other similar efforts.

As a preliminary integration piece, coaches should support coachees in focusing on a project that can be easily accomplished within a reasonable time frame. This will support coached teachers in rapidly recognizing the advantages of incorporating digital tools and resources in the classroom, and this will likely offer a confidence boost as well as increased inspiration to tackle more difficult projects.

Once coachees have accomplished smaller achievements in integrating technology for increased personal and professional productivity, coaches might then begin to transition them from teacher-centered to student-centered technological applications. When determining next projects to undertake, coaches and coached teachers must remain mindful of this simple yet important motto: "Content is king!" Before deciding upon the tool or methodology to be employed, coaching partners should initially focus on the content to be delivered. This will provide heightened purpose behind integration activities and will also result in a more pertinent and meaningful final product.

As coaches seek to support their coached teachers in integrating new technological tools or resources, they should employ modeling whenever feasible. Significant research endeavors have exhibited that modeling is an impactful instructional strategy in that it provides learners the opportunity to explore an instructor's thought processes. According to social learning theorist Albert Bandura (1977), "Learning would be exceedingly laborious, not to mention hazardous, if people had to rely solely on the effects of their own actions to inform them what to do. Fortunately, most human behavior is learned observationally through modeling: from observing others one forms an idea of how new behaviors are performed, and on later occasions this coded information serves as a guide for action" (p. 2).

Every day, countless educators effectively integrate modeling to boost student learning throughout disciplines and across a variety of grade levels. Similarly, coaches can use modeling to support fellow colleagues in incorporating instructional technology in their own classroom learning contexts.

Within the above-mentioned collegial coaching case studies, the power of project-based learning surfaced as a prevalent, foundational theme. In certain cases, after meeting and deciding upon the content to address, the coaching pairs still felt unsure regarding the most appropriate technological resources to incorporate with students. In these situations, two occurrences ensued: First, coaches candidly conveyed their uncertainty regarding the most effective course of action, and second, coaches in these circumstances offered to conduct further research and report back to their coachees regarding possible solutions.

Such situations seemed to emphasize the notion that both the coach and the coached teacher were consistently learning in partnership. This also suggested to the coached teacher that integrating digital tools and resources is not always a straightforward process. In fact, effective technology implementation cannot typically be accomplished without an investment of time, energy, and reflection.

In some cases—especially when a coach partnered with a coachee outside of his or her content area specialization—even extensive research conducted by the coach did not necessarily lead to the answers needed. On such occasions, the coach was encouraged to seek support from other coaches within the graduate class setting to brainstorm applicable technological tools. For administrators supported by teams of coaches on a school campus, brainstorming with other coaches could take place in this setting.

This collective brainstorming method helped guarantee that no one was left to solve integration problems in solitude. Thus, all coaches and coachees involved in the process were provided one or more colleagues to rely upon for collaborative support in thinking through various ideas.

Phase 4: Assess the Progress

Assessment signifies a key component of any collegial coaching program, principally because it supports coaches and coached teachers in deciding whether the goals of coaching are being accomplished (progress in both technology integration and student-centered instructional practices). Evaluation processes influence decisions about coaching needs and the path that future coaching experiences should take. It also encourages coaches to ask these essential questions:

- Am I teaching what I intend to teach?
- Is my coachee accomplishing the goals and finishing the projects on which we decided to focus?
- Is there a more effective method of teaching this concept, thereby promoting greater involvement by learners and more consistent student success?

Coaches and coached teachers must thoughtfully consider the time and effort involved in learning new concepts or skills. Additionally, they must evaluate which partners accomplished which tasks, taking the coachees' level of dependence into account through each step of the project. Ideally, coached teachers should become gradually less dependent upon their coaches over time, directly relating to their growing capabilities and confidence levels.

When used within the collegial coaching process, assessment takes on any number of formats. This may include both formative and summative assessment, and it may also be performed either informally or formally. It is critical that assessment occur at each milestone for the coach and coachee—throughout the planning stages, in the midst of the integration process, and at the point of accomplishing of each goal.

In fact, every time a coach and coached teacher conference together, both partners should evaluate the progress toward accomplishing the final product. The coach should assess the needs of the coached teacher while offering new opportunities for technology integration tools and methods. Concurrently, the coachee should evaluate the options shared by the coach, seeking to ascertain the most fitting solutions to meet the needs of the students.

When formative assessment opportunities arise throughout the planning process, both the coach and the coachee should evaluate the existing resources and possible implementation schedules. Additionally, the coach and the coached teacher might develop rubrics by which to assess student-created products. Once the implementation takes place, evaluation moves from formative to summative assessment processes. Summative assessments are primarily addressed in the next stage, which focuses upon reflection.

Phase 5: Reflect on the Integration

As in any worthwhile undertaking, reflection comprises a critical element for success within the collegial coaching process. Over many years, reflection has time and time again been noted as an essential teaching practice by educational researchers (Dewey, 1933; Langley & Senne, 1997).

Reflective educators do not shy away from contemplating the good, the bad, and the ugly. They dedicate time and energy to carefully contemplating questions such as the following:

- Which elements of this experience went well?
- Which elements did not unfold as intended?
- What might be handled differently next time?
- What changes should be made to this situation?

The coach and coachee should collaborate in reflecting upon and searching for answers to a variety of questions focusing upon student learning, including:

- What new knowledge and skills did the students learn from this endeavor?
- Did they accomplish more or less than they have in previous lessons without technology?
- What elements should be modified for next time?
- What was the most effective aspect of this integration piece?
- What was the most difficult aspect of this integration piece?
- How might this same digital tool or resource be incorporated within another unit or lesson?
- In what ways did the students demonstrate higher-order thinking skills?
- In what ways did the students achieve new levels of knowledge and comprehension pertaining to this project?
- In what ways was student motivation impacted by this integration piece?

Over time, coaches and coached teachers should search out new goals on which to focus; and in doing so, they should also remain cognizant of the need to carefully evaluate the progress attained at various points throughout the process for teachers and students. Additionally, time and effort should regularly be dedicated to reflection, as this represents a vital ingredient for significant and enduring change.

In reexamining these phases of the coaching process, coaches and coached teachers set themselves up for accomplishing even greater success. The more experience educators acquire in undertaking new technology implementation challenges, reviewing their progress, and contemplating their efforts, the higher their confidence skyrockets and the more their students ultimately profit, both academically and technologically speaking.

ESSENTIAL IDEAS TO REMEMBER

Nearly anyone with a sense of technological expertise can remember a time when a friend, colleague, or family member needed support in accomplishing a task or finding a solution involving a technological difficulty. In such cases, there is often a strong temptation to provide a "quick fix" without devoting the time to expound upon the steps to a solution. Yet, one might logically presume that the next time a similar issue presents itself, a similar situation will arise.

As time and effort are dedicated to guiding the struggling individual in solving comparable problems, so grows the probability of more independent future problem-solving endeavors. This line of thinking translates to the practice of guiding educators as they address real-world, professionally significant technology integration challenges.

As the saying goes, "Give a man a fish, and you feed him for a day; show him how to catch fish, and you feed him for a lifetime." As this proverbial expression implies, the process of acquiring a new skill encompasses infinitely greater value than a one-off handout. This line of reasoning closely correlates with the process of guiding an educator in learning to meaningfully integrate technology. The limitless dividends produced by this investment greatly overshadow the time and energy invested, impacting teachers and their students for years to come.

REFERENCES

Alaniz, K., & Wilson, D. (2015). *Naturalizing digital immigrants: The power of collegial coaching for technology integration.* Lanham, MD: Rowman & Littlefield Education.

Bandura, A. (1977). *Social learning theory.* New York, NY: General Learning Press.

Bland, C., Taylor, A. L., Shollen, S. L., Weber-Main, A. M., and Mulcahy, P. A. (2009). *Faculty success through mentoring: A guide for mentors, mentees, and leaders.* Lanham, MD: Rowman & Littlefield Education.

Dewey, J. (1933). *How we think: A restatement of the relation of reflective thinking to the educative process.* Chicago, IL: D.C. Heath.

Fibkins, W. L. (2011). *An administrator's guide to teacher mentoring.* Lanham, MD: Rowman & Littlefield Education.

Herring, M. C., Koehler, M. J., & Mishra, P. (2016). *Handbook of technological pedagogical content knowledge (TPACK) for educators* (2nd ed.). New York, NY: Routledge.

Howland, J., Jonassen, D., & Marra, R. (2012). *Meaningful learning with technology* (4th ed.). New York, NY: Pearson Education.

Knight, J. (2007). *Instructional Coaching : A partnership approach to improving instruction.* Thousand Oaks, CA: Corwin Press.

Knight, J. (2011). What good coaches do. *Educational Learning, 69*(2), 18–22.

Koehler, M. J., & Mishra, P. (2009). What is technological pedagogical content knowledge? *Contemporary Issues in Technology and Teacher Education,* 9(1). Retrieved from www.citejournal.org/vol9/iss1/general/article1.cfm

Kopcha, T. (2010). A systems-based approach to technology integration using mentoring and communities of practice. *Educational Technology Research and Development, 58*(2), 175–90.

Langley, D. J., & Senne, T. (1997). Telling the stories of teaching: Reflective writing for preservice teachers. *Journal of Physical Education, Recreation & Dance, 68*(8), 56–60.

Lei, J., & Zhao, Y. (2007) Technology uses and student achievement: A longitudinal study. *Computers in Education, 49,* 284–96. Retrieved from http://www.gram.edu/sacs/qep/chapter%206/6_8Lei.pdf

McCrary, N., & Mazur, J. (2010). Conceptualizing a narrative simulation to promote dialogic reflection: Using a multiple outcome design to engage teacher mentors. *Educational Technology Research and Development, 58*(3), 325–42.

Mishra, P. (2008). *Handbook of TPCK AACTE Committee on Innovation and Technology.* New York, NY: Routledge.

Wilson, D., Brupbacher, L., Simpson, C., & Alaniz, K. (2013). Naturalizing digital immigrants: Technology integration and implications for teacher professional development. *Texas Study of Secondary Education, 22*(2), 36–40.

Chapter Four

First Responders of Professional Development

"Leaders become great not because of their power, but because of their ability to empower others."—John Maxwell

Aristotle famously asserted that "the whole is greater than the sum of its parts." The validity of this principle can be seen across various circumstances and contexts. For instance, imagine a modest, rigid cluster of graphite, seemingly not much more than a simple collection of carbon atoms. However, when graphite encounters tremendous pressure over an extended period of time, it ultimately becomes a diamond, the most unyielding—and many would say stunning—material on the earth. This example reflects one of nature's best illustrations of the whole's greatness in comparison to than sum of various parts.

In some respects, cultivating excellent collegial coaches within educational settings parallels the process of creating diamonds. The success of any collegial coaching program is directly related to the quality of its varying elements, including available resources. The time and consideration devoted to planning, the digital tools at teachers' and students' disposal, the buy-in from school leadership, and countless other programmatic components exemplify significant concerns. However, the quality of the collegial coaches involved quite possibly represents the most crucial of these elements. Unless excellent coaches are involved, the probability of a quality collegial coaching program is nearly nonexistent.

In fact, within the Coaching CPR Method, collegial coaches exemplify the "first responders" of professional development. Their expertise, provided in a timely and efficient manner, holds the potential to resuscitate lifeless instructional technology integration endeavors. Just as first responders rush to the site of emergencies equipped with life-saving knowledge, skills, and expertise, collegial coaches deliver just-in-time expertise and applicable tools to revive curricular and instructional endeavors. They breathe new life into programs that seem to be weakening under the restrictive pressures of mounting demands for accountability and encouragement to "teach to the tests."

Methods of developing excellent first responders of professional development may seem straightforward. However, this can be quite an involved process. Quality collegial coaches are unique and should be highly valued by their organizations. In truth, a perfect blueprint does not exist for creating outstanding coaches, and this chapter is not intended to provide readers with a cut-and-dried formula. Even still, a program's success in cultivating a network of coaches greater than the sum of its parts is, to some extent, reflective of the leadership guiding the program. This chapter provides a roadmap for educational administrators as they work to identify and develop exceptional coaches from within their school settings.

Coaches with expertise in incorporating digital tools and resources guide the learning and attainment of new technological skills by fellow educators. This relationship signifies a professional development medium through which teachers may begin to incorporate instructional technology with success.

COLLEGIAL COACHES TO THE RESCUE

In the book *Leadership Mentoring*, Gross (2006) highlights several distinctive characteristics that exceptional mentors share. This chapter highlights a number of these unique qualities, uncovered both as a result of coaching case studies as well as during research focusing upon leadership and collegial coaching. Within the case studies described in the previous chapter (Alaniz & Wilson, 2015), graduate students drawing near to the conclusion of the collegial coaching experience offered their perspectives regarding the traits of an excellent coach.

Nathan, a coach in a private school setting, shared the following thoughts: "The ideal coach needs to be a well informed and knowledgeable in pedagogy and best practices. He or she must be willing and able to learn about other content areas and disciplines, and he or she should enjoy researching and exploring new ideas." Furthermore, "a coach should be an experienced, excellent classroom teacher because he or she must apply ideas, concepts, strategies, and resources to a real classroom in a practical way. Coaches should also be optimistic and realistic, capable of developing a vision and setting goals for other teachers. Most importantly, the coach should practice humility and genuinely seek to meet the needs of the teacher."

Quality coaches demonstrate characteristics of change leadership. Research and functional insight support the idea that exceptional educational leaders must have experience as educators (Tichy, 2009). Excellent coaches bring expertise from serving within a classroom setting. Not only should they have directly guided learners within an educational context, but they should also maintain the mindset of lifelong learners. Suitable candidates for coaching nurture a personal desire to learn novel concepts and a commitment to dedicate the time and energy needed to accomplish this pursuit.

Furthermore, exceptional coaches possess the courage to step beyond their comfort zones into entirely new experiences. They instinctively desire to think outside of the box, to challenge and extend their original assumptions, and to grow as individuals and as professionals though every phase of the journey. Moreover, exceptional coaches experience joy and enthusiasm as they achieve inroads that inspire others to tackle new learning endeavors and developmental goals.

As quality coaches embrace opportunities for growth, they discover strategies for redirecting negativity or other obstacles to progress that may present themselves along the way. Such coaches intentionally encourage themselves to remember that hesitation or pushback from others is often not personal. Instead, those resistant to change involving unfamiliar experiences may be hindered by doubts and lack of confidence. Effective coaches keep the faith in the face of barriers that crop up along the way. They maintain an optimistic belief that these obstacles can be overcome and view each challenge as a prospective occasion for development and progress forward.

THE COLLECTIVE POWER OF TECHNOLOGICAL INNOVATION AND TEACHING EXCELLENCE

Quality coaches demonstrate proficiency in technological applications and pedagogical skill (from both teacher-centered and student-centered perspectives). Moreover, their aptitude in these areas must be apparent to those who serve within their professional contexts. A teacher who intuitively and steadily displays skill as an instructor as well as effectiveness at technological integration will naturally earn greater credibility as a coach among colleagues.

To expand the proficiency of collegial coaches engaged in coaching case studies, the graduate students participating in the process completed prerequisite courses focusing upon acquisition of meaningful technology integration strategies. Throughout these courses, they gained experience with comprehensively incorporating digital tools and resources within their chosen content areas. The student coaches planned for instructional endeavors incorporating multimedia, data manipulation applications, website design resources, and online collaboration tools for student and teacher productivity, among other tools and applications.

Additionally, they often viewed presentations and tutorials designed by fellow students in the program, thus allowing them to learn from others integrating technology outside of the content areas and grade levels with which they were accustomed. Engaging in such activities supported the coaches in visualizing applications for digital tools and resources throughout various developmental levels and disciplines. Over time, the coaches collaborated in cultivating a database of ideas for technology applications within various educational contexts.

KEYS TO COACHING IN TODAY'S DIGITAL AGE

As technological developments and applications expand within educational environments—as well as in countless other aspects of daily life—collegial coaches must consistently formulate new strategies for supporting fellow colleagues in hitting the ever-shifting target of effective instruction within the digital age. They should intentionally focus upon encouraging, supporting, and guiding coached teachers in embracing the incredible potential of technological innovations, remaining mindful of the fact that not every lesson must incorporate technology to be effective. Digital tools and resources should be incorporated with purpose and intentionality, and effective coaches support teachers in doing so.

Quality coaches acknowledge that in an age of rapid technological advancement, simply being able to operate digital tools and resources is not enough. Today's coaches must assertively and adeptly guide coached teachers in applying technology to discover unconventional strategies for conveying content to learners, design innovative means of engaging them, and creating interactive authentic assessment methods.

The International Society for Technology in Education provides a set of seven essential standards for coaches to successfully support teachers as they prepare their students to flourish within a progressively more global, digital world. "Change agent" tops this list; more specifically, coaches of the digital age "inspire educators and leaders to use technology to create equitable and ongoing access to high-quality learning" (ISTE, 2019).

Change Agent

As change agents, collegial coaches cultivate a common vision and culture for implementing digital tools and resources to hasten transformation via coaching endeavors. They encourage the equitable incorporation of technological tools and content to address the needs of every student. They establish an encouraging culture of coaching that supports teachers and educational administrators in reaching a shared vision and identifying personalized goals. Such coaches unite problem solvers, content experts, instructional support personnel, technical support staff, teachers, and administrators to expand the potential of digital tools and resources to enhance learning endeavors.

Connected Learner

In addition to operating as change agents, exceptional collegial coaches also serve as connected learners. According to the ISTE (2019) guidelines for coaches of the digital age, successful technology coaches "model the ISTE Standards for Students and the ISTE Standards for Educators and identify ways to improve their coaching practice."

In seeking to address these fundamental goals, excellent coaches pursue learning experiences that expand their expertise in the ISTE standards, thus serving as models to teachers and educational leaders.

They engage in professional learning networks in order to develop as coaches and to keep in step with innovative pedagogical methods, instructional technology, and the learning sciences. Furthermore, they collaboratively develop goals with coached teachers, reflect upon successful endeavors, and seek to continuously heighten coaching and teaching methods.

Collaborator

Beyond functioning as change agents and connected leaders, insightful coaches also serve as effective collaborators. In doing so, they "establish productive relationships with educators in order to improve instructional practice and learning outcomes" (ISTE, 2019). Through these relationships, they support teachers in investigating novel pedagogical strategies.

Additionally, they work alongside educators to incorporate digital tools and resources that are applicable, developmentally fitting for students, and closely associated with content standards. They team up with teachers to assess the effectiveness of digitally based content to provide insights regarding the implementation of technological tools and resources. Furthermore, they offer guidance for teachers by designing and demonstrating helpful strategies for incorporating innovative digital tools and resources into teaching practices.

Learning Designer

As outlined in the ISTE (2019) standards, quality coaches "model and support educators to design learning experiences and environments to meet the needs and interests of all students." They work alongside other educators to design authentic, student-centered learning endeavors that cultivate student agency, deepen learners' mastery of content, and provide students with the opportunity to demonstrate the knowledge and skills they have acquired. They support teachers in using digital tools to create meaningful assessments, offer timely input, and foster individualized learning. Furthermore, they partner with educators to create engaging learning environments and model the application of instructional design strategies to produce effective digital learning settings.

Professional Learning Facilitator

In this digital age, successful coaches "plan, provide, and evaluate the impact of professional learning for educators and leaders to use technology to advance teaching and learning" (ISTE, 2019). They tailor professional development experiences to address the needs of the teachers they coach in accordance with needs assessments and proven methods for supporting adult learning. They help educators, educational leaders, and instructional teams to apply the ISTE standards by leading active learning experiences and offering valuable feedback. Furthermore, they assess the impact of professional development opportunities and resultant learning, constantly seeking to improve such experiences in order to address the campus-wide vision for teaching and learning endeavors.

Data-Driven Decision Maker

Excellent collegial coaches seek to "model and support the use of qualitative and quantitative data to inform their own instruction and professional learning" (ISTE, 2019). In doing so, they support teachers and administrators in securely obtaining and evaluating data. Additionally, they guide colleagues in interpreting data that is both qualitative and quantitative in nature, allowing them to make increasingly informed decisions that benefit individual students' learning experiences. Furthermore, they collaborate with educators to empower students to apply data in developing personalized learning goals and gauging progress toward those goals.

Digital Citizen Advocate

The final coaching standard presented by ISTE (2019) involves coaches' endeavors to "model digital citizenship and support educators and students in recognizing the responsibilities and opportunities inherent in living in a digital world." Quality collegial coaches faithfully encourage and inspire teachers and their students to apply digital tools and resources to pursuits involving community improvement. They partner with educational stakeholders to build a culture of respect in online interactions as well as helpful, healthy boundaries regarding technology use. They guide teachers and their students in reflectively evaluating online media sources. Finally, they empower administrators, educators, and learners to make wise decisions in the interest of protecting personal information and curating the digital footprint they desire to project.

THE PRICELESS WORTH OF A STERLING REPUTATION

As previously highlighted, a solid reputation for excellence in teaching and technology integration provides trustworthiness regarding a coach's capabilities. Even still, a coach's reputation should extend beyond skill in successfully fostering innovative learning and technological implementation endeavors. A quality coach must cultivate a sterling reputation, both professionally and personally, as this is essential for building trust among colleagues.

Excellent collegial coaches not only possess exceptional content knowledge, but they also display an "infectious personality," thereby inspiring teachers in their pursuit enhance their professional practices (Steiner & Kowal, 2007). Lindsay, a graduate student coach serving on a middle school campus, observed that "coaches must be people with large servants' hearts, unafraid to lead or invest in another person."

Unless colleagues place confidence in the coaches selected to guide them, it is highly unlikely that they will readily share concerns, questions, and needs regarding technology integration. Trust represents a vital first step in inviting a colleague into one's professional and personal spheres, particularly when a steep learning curve is involved. Successful relationships are established upon a foundation of trust, and this includes coaching partnerships within school settings.

After trust is firmly established, the coached teacher is much more likely to confess setbacks to their coach, encouraged by the assurance that this information will be kept between the coach and coachee. Only at that point can the challenge be gradually and productively addressed. Through individualized, nonevaluative encounters, trust is eventually established; step by step, the coached teacher begins to rely upon the coach for support that extends beyond surface-level needs.

The art of establishing genuine trust requires that coaches earn the respect of colleagues over time through displaying traits such as sincerity, reliability, and an evident desire to go beyond the call of duty. Coaches who win this type of deep respect begin to develop an exceptional reputation. They are viewed as individuals who place their professional character on the line each day, unfailingly seeking not simply to meet, but instead to exceed, colleagues' expectations.

When describing the value of a solid reputation, Socrates sagely advised,

> Regard your good name as the richest jewel you can possibly be possessed of—for credit is like fire; when once you have kindled it you may easily preserve it, but if you once extinguish it, you will find it an arduous task to rekindle it again. The way to a good reputation is to endeavor to be what you desire to appear.

Because collegial respect is earned over time and as a result of consistent, conscientious effort, it is beneficial when collegial coaches are chosen from campus settings at which they have been teaching for a significant period of time. In many cases, faculty members are more likely to trust colleagues with whom they already have a working relationship.

Sometimes, when instructional leaders are brought to a new educational context from the external professional world, it may take a bit longer to establish trust in their character and capabilities. However, in instances where this seems the only practical choice, effective coaching endeavors are certainly still feasible. Through consistently demonstrating revered personal and professional traits like those mentioned previously, new collegial coaches will steadily secure the confidence and esteem of their fellow colleagues.

THE PROMISE OF POSITIVE FEEDBACK

Exceptional coaches leverage opportunities to offer encouragement and celebrate success. Positive feedback emphasizes the value of work well done and elevates coachees' self-confidence and desire to press forward in accomplishing identified goals. Teachers frequently witness the incredible power of effectively shared encouragement as they engage with learners within their own classrooms. Principles used to provide students with positive feedback can also be efficaciously applied within coaching relationships.

Successful coaches intentionally shape their encouragement regarding coachees' progress as a strategy for increasing teachers' motivation. For example, praise that specifically describes notable growth in incorporating instructional technology may be especially helpful. Comments such as, "Well done!" often fall short, as they lack specificity regarding progress (Hawkins & Heflin, 2011). On the other hand, statements of encouragement become more significant when extended to highlight an explicit action taken, such as, "You effectively incorporated the collaborative tool we discussed, and your students were evidently engaged throughout your lesson today. Well done!"

Moreover, exceptional coaches identify methods for communicating their coachees' dedication and achievements, rather than solely concentrating on their level of skill in terms of technology integration. For instance, a coach might note, "The time and effort you dedicated to incorporating this student-centered app into your unit is definitely reaping significant benefits. Your students' excitement over this project is a testament to your diligent work."

Wise coaches share their coached teachers' successes with administrators. Many teachers greatly value opportunities to accomplish something notable in the eyes of their supervisor, and progress with a collegial coach is no exception. Most employees intuitively appreciate and flourish as a result of positive feedback from leadership, and such encouragement may even motivate dedication to further progress.

However, challenges or failures are typically best kept between the coached teacher and the coach. Just as teachers may thrive on a word of encouragement from an administrator, they may wither as a result of failures aired in the presence of a supervisor. Discretion and simple measures of kindness and respect toward the coachee will accomplish tremendous steps forward in fostering a respectful, nonthreatening environment for progress.

Finally, coaches should seek to support their coachees in showcasing student projects that involve meaningful technology integration. These partnerships should advertise the exceptional work learners accomplish. For instance, a coach might guide the coached teacher in using the school's website to display students' digital artifacts of learning, begin a faculty meeting with a quick show-and-tell, commence a parent conference or open house by displaying student work, and so on. The sky is the limit!

The self-confidence and enthusiasm generated as a result of intentional, sincere encouragement is contagious. Teachers frequently communicate with each other, thus promoting the sharing of successes. Genuine celebrations of substantial achievements create ripple effects throughout a campus community. As a coached teacher accomplishes personally significant goals or successfully incorporates new technologies, feelings of greater expertise naturally arise. These triumphs should be shared with others!

Excellent coaches play a key role in celebrating these victories. Throughout this process, they also reinforce the importance of sharing their knowledge and skills with colleagues, thus extending the collegial coaching cycle. Before too long, those teachers who informally engaged in the coaching process will start to communicate with colleagues about successful projects. Activities such as this build confidence in teachers, opening new doors of opportunity for effective technology integration.

THE IDEAL LEADER?

This chapter highlights various qualities of excellent collegial coaches. These qualities include a wide range of abilities as well as personal and professional characteristics. If any one individual were capable of unceasingly demonstrating all of these traits, this person would undoubtedly embody the "ideal leader." Yet, in reflecting upon these qualities, it is important to remain mindful of the fact that in real life, the ideal leader does not exist.

Within any circumstance or context, a leader will undeniably experience missteps. Every leader is ultimately only human, and as such, is developing along the way. Furthermore, if an educational community's conception of leadership is based on the expectation of flawlessness, this limited and unrealistic perspective will almost certainly lead to frustration and disillusionment.

An expectation of perfection in any setting is unwise, mainly because it cannot practically be applied to a genuine framework for leadership or coaching. Although the perfect coach does not exist, humble coaches do. Moreover, a coach's humility when facing imperfect moments might ultimately signify exceptional leadership. In everyday life as well as in coaching contexts, humility offers an initial foundation for productive, innovative, and lasting growth.

Humble leaders truly shine in a world in which self-promotion and looking out for number one is both supported and admired. In a dog-eat-dog society, humble leaders possess the tremendous power to bring about positive impact in their communities. In today's world, so many long for and feel genuinely inspired by servant leaders who exemplify the unique, priceless trait of sincere humility.

By accepting criticism and remaining open to mistakes, humble collegial coaches welcome opportunities for professional and personal growth. In doing so, such coaches inspire growth in those within their spheres of influence. Just as excellent coaches make the most of opportunities to celebrate achievements, they also find value in embracing and learning as a result of failure. In fact, they recognize that the most meaningful victories are sometimes achieved in, and even because of, past failures.

John C. Maxwell, a globally recognized leadership authority, speaker, author, and coach, shares these words of wisdom for leaders within various contexts, including collegial coaches: "Know that you're going to make mistakes. The fellow who never makes a mistake takes his orders from one who does. Wake up and realize this: Failure is simply a price we pay to achieve success." In so many instances, the road to leadership success may be discovered through adopting a clear-cut yet profound motto: "Fail early, fail often, but always fail forward" (Maxwell, 2007).

ESSENTIAL IDEAS TO REMEMBER

With regard to instructional technology use, excellent collegial coaches possess invaluable experiences, knowledge, and skills that distinctively position them to deeply impact the technological integration endeavors of fellow educators. Collegial coaching offers a professional helping relationship whereby an invested, experienced coach supports a colleague's acquisition of vital instructional skills for the digital age. When effectively implemented, collegial coaching programs serve to remove a burden from coached colleagues as they receive differentiated guidance in meeting the needs of today's learners.

Impactful collegial coaches are made—not born—as they welcome, learn alongside, and even grow as a result of their own failures. The characteristics of effective coaches often develop gradually over time. Furthermore, each discovery along the way brings them closer and closer to making an enduring impact upon the educators and learners within their school contexts.

REFERENCES

Alaniz, K., & Wilson, D. (2015). *Naturalizing digital immigrants: The power of collegial coaching for technology integration.* Lanham, MD: Rowman & Littlefield Education.

Gross, S. J. (2006). *Leadership mentoring: Maintaining school improvement in turbulent times.* Lanham, MD: Rowman & Littlefield Education.

Hawkins, S. M., & Heflin, L. J. (2011). Increasing secondary teachers' behavior-specific praise using a video self-modeling and visual performance feedback intervention. *Journal of Positive Behavior Interventions, 13*(2) 97–108.

International Society for Technology in Education (2019). *Standards•C.* Retrieved from https://www.iste.org/standards/for-coaches

Maxwell, J. C. (2007). *Failing forward: Turning mistakes into stepping stones for success.* Nashville, TN: Thomas Nelson.

Steiner, L., & Kowal, J. (2007). *Instructional coaching.* Washington, DC: Center for Comprehensive School Reform and Improvement.

Tichy, N. M. (2009). *The cycle of leadership.* New York, NY: Harper Collins.

Chapter Five

The Urgency of Content-Focused Coaching

> *"To begin with the end in mind means to start with a clear understanding of your destination. It means to know where you're going so that you better understand where you are now and so that the steps you take are always in the right direction."* —Steven R. Covey

In his enduring, oft-quoted book *The 7 Habits of Highly Effective People: Restoring the Character Ethic,* Covey (1989) provides an overview of life principles that effectively translate to countless personal and professional undertakings. One of these principles, Habit 2, highlights the importance of beginning with the end in mind. This significance of this practice applies to each aspect of the Coaching CPR Method, and particularly the *C* in CPR, or the focus upon content within collegial coaching practices.

Wise individuals plan new journeys in life by first considering the destination. Yogi Berra, an American baseball player who amassed a number of famous quotes throughout his lifetime, once remarked, "If you don't know where you're going, you'll end up someplace else." Along similar lines, Antoine de Saint-Exupéry, a French writer, poet, journalist, and pioneering aviator, simply remarked, "A goal without a plan is a wish." Without an end in mind, there is little sense in beginning the journey.

The notion of beginning with the end in mind parallels Simon Sinek's now highly recognized principle, "Start with why." In his inspirational book, entitled *Start with Why: How Great Leaders Inspire Everyone to Take Action*, Sinek contends that although most organizations can easily explain *what* they do and some can also describe *how* they are unique or better, few can clearly communicate *why* they do what they do.

Sinek (2011) explains,

> Knowing your WHY is not the only way to be successful, but it is the only way to maintain a lasting success and have a greater blend of innovation and flexibility. When a WHY goes fuzzy, it becomes much more difficult to maintain the growth, loyalty and inspiration that helped drive the original success. By difficult, I mean that manipulation rather than inspiration fast becomes the strategy of choice to motivate behavior. This is effective in the short term but comes at a high cost in the long term. (p. 50)

Collegial coaches, much like leaders in any organizational setting, more naturally maintain long-term success and motivate innovation by remaining mindful of the "why." They inspire lasting growth from teachers and their students, as well as improved leadership and faculty buy-in—even from those who were once hesitant to engage in coaching endeavors. Coaches must clearly identify the destination before starting the journey, and the preceding chapters discuss research and experiences that build a solid case for the "why" behind collegial coaching for professional development.

Like coaches, teachers who begin with the end in mind and remain mindful of the "why" inspire genuine student engagement and impactful learning experiences. When educators develop a clear vision for where students should arrive prior to commencing new learning journeys, the likelihood that students will take action to reach this destination increases significantly. Henry Wong, a longtime educator, insightful author, and sought-after speaker on teaching effectiveness, explains, "In an effective classroom, students should not only know what they are doing, they should also know why and how."

Unfortunately, far too many educational systems, and the teachers within them, pack each day with busywork that fails to bring students closer to the overarching goals and corresponding objectives. Many educators unknowingly become so caught up in daily to-do lists that they have little time left to think about the purpose behind their work or the tasks at which their students are laboring away each day. In cases such as this, teachers and their students might begin to feel as though they are traveling down a path without purpose; journeys without the "why" eventually begin to seem murky and arduous.

Countless educators—and, as a result, their students—would be greatly encouraged to collaborate with a collegial coach skilled at helping them reflect upon a meaningful destination. Such coaches serve as bright lights to break through the haze and illuminate the path toward the ultimate point of arrival.

In the Coaching CPR Method, effective coaches take time from the outset to support teachers in pondering and answering questions such as the following:

- Why are you teaching this unit?
- Why are you passionate about this content?
- Beyond answers such as, "This content is mandated by the state or district," why is this unit or lesson important for students to learn?
- Why should students care about learning this content?

Once a teacher supported by a collegial coach has actively reflected upon "why"-centric questions like those above, the pair should begin focusing on other destination-oriented questions. The following examples guide teachers in beginning with the end in mind:

- What overarching goals should students achieve through this unit?
- What corresponding objectives should students grasp through this unit?
- What artifacts of learning might students create to demonstrate that they have mastered the knowledge and skills addressed within these goals and objectives?

Once teachers attain a clearer vision for the purpose of the journey and the destination to be reached, they can more effectively navigate the road ahead. Rather than focusing as much time and attention to their daily "to do's," a collegial coach can support them in achieving a meaningful sense of purpose to fuel them as they venture toward their destination.

These principles of "begin with the end in mind" and "start with why" provide power and purpose in curriculum mapping endeavors. Although instructional and technological innovations come and go, successful coaches and the teachers they support remain mindful of this tried-and-true maxim: "Content is king!"

Intentional, effective planning entails first deciding upon an applicable curricular design model. While a number of frameworks for curriculum development exist, those highlighted in this chapter have been demonstrated as effective options over time through various research studies and within diverse educational contexts.

THE UNDERSTANDING BY DESIGN FRAMEWORK

Created by Jay McTighe and Grant Wiggins (2012), the Understanding by Design framework offers a proven, efficacious means by which to establish planning procedures for teaching and learning. Some key principles of this model include the following:

1. Learning endeavors are enhanced when educators purposefully contemplate curricular planning.
2. In curriculum design and teaching, focus should be placed on the elevation and extension of student understanding, as well as their ability to transfer learning to future pursuits (for example, the ability to meaningfully employ content knowledge and corresponding skills).
3. Understanding is revealed when students receive opportunities to autonomously make sense of new learning, eventually demonstrating acquired knowledge and skills through real-world applications.
4. Effective curriculum planning incorporates a framework known as "backward design."

    a. First, educators should identify desired results for their students. Through the process, the following preliminary questions should be contemplated: Ultimately, what should learners know and be able to do? Along these same lines, which overarching standards must be addressed?
    b. Teachers should also establish a set of learning goals to work toward. This includes pinpointing key enduring understandings that will remain with students long after the lesson or unit has concluded.
    c. Educators must also consider what evidence of learning students will be required to demonstrate. The identified evidence of learning should entail specific strat-

egies for evaluating the extent to which students have acquired necessary knowledge and skills.
d. Finally, a plan for learning must be developed. This plan should encourage teachers and their students to begin with the end in mind; this road map will serve as a guide toward achieving the ultimate destination, or the goals established from the outset.

When implemented effectively, the Understanding by Design framework supports teachers and their students in avoiding common roadblocks that frequently occur in many classroom settings. For instance, it steers them away from viewing the textbook as the curriculum instead of as simply a curricular resource. Furthermore, it offers a viable solution to the absence of overarching purpose and clear-cut priorities common within activity-oriented classroom endeavors.

Ultimately, the Understanding by Design framework guides educators and the collegial coaches who support them in placing first things first. Through this time-tested method, student-centered, meaningful, lifelong learning occurs. Those who implement this model position themselves to provide countless opportunities for meaning making and real-world application for learning in a variety of educational contexts.

THE UNIVERSAL DESIGN FOR LEARNING (UDL) MODEL

Universal Design for Learning (UDL) is an alternative method of curriculum planning that highlights flexibility and the provision of alternatives in content delivery and assessment practices. Backed by extensive research, UDL embodies a significant framework for supporting academic practices that focus on several critical goals. Specifically, it offers flexibility in strategies for presenting content to students. Moreover, it provides various options for student engagement in the learning process, responses to instruction, and demonstration of new knowledge and skills.

The UDL framework reduces instructional obstacles, offering appropriate accommodations and challenging learners through detailing high expectations for all students. Teachers are encouraged to provide various methods of content representation for learners. Moreover, UDL challenges educators to offer students a variety of opportunities for expression, including both tangible and communicative action. Additionally, this framework fosters numerous strategies for engagement, all of which are designed to encourage inquisitiveness, persistence, and self-regulation from students.

BLOOM'S TAXONOMY

Any curricular planning endeavor should focus upon the knowledge and skills students must ultimately apply in real-world settings as well as approaches for achieving identified learning goals. A foundational basis for curricular design, Bloom's taxonomy highlights the actions through which learners express their understanding of and ability to apply acquired content to practical settings.

Bloom's taxonomy, which was created by Dr. Benjamin Bloom in 1956, serves as a straightforward classification process for various learning objectives teachers may set for students. Preferably, this classification method should be incorporated throughout instructional and learning cycles as students acquire the content in increasingly complex ways. Distinguishing key, diverse learning goals or objectives aligns with the process of identifying desired results in the Understanding by Design framework. At this point, teachers decide what students should eventually know and be able to do.

Learning at higher levels of the taxonomy is dependent on having attained prerequisite knowledge and skills at lower levels. A goal of effective instruction involves moving students from the lower levels of the taxonomy to the higher levels in order to encompass true content area learning.

The levels are as follows:

- Remembering: recalling basic facts, concepts, and answers
- Understanding: comparing, interpreting, or providing descriptions and key ideas
- Applying: solving problems in new situations by using acquired facts, techniques, and rules pertaining to the content at hand
- Analyzing: formulating inferences and generalizations about the topic while relating it to previously learned content
- Evaluating: validating ideas, making judgements, and defending perspectives based on criteria and evidence pertaining to content
- Creating: restructuring content into a novel pattern or framework

Teachers may easily get lost amid the many available digital tools and resources for learning, not sure how best to incorporate them in engaging tech-savvy learners. This is why collegial coaches who can effectively navigate curriculum design frameworks along with applicable technologies are so vital in today's educational contexts. Not every lesson must include digital tools and resources. In fact, selecting technological tools and trying to make them fit within a unit or lesson is a prime example of placing the cart before the horse, as the saying goes.

Curricular frameworks—along with a focus upon content—should come first, and incorporation of the appropriate digital tools and resources should then follow as applicable. This simplifies the technology integration process considerably, allowing teachers to leverage technology as a tool to address learning objectives rather than as a vehicle driving the educational experience.

ESSENTIAL IDEAS TO REMEMBER

Effective planning for technology integration might understandably seem somewhat overwhelming for today's teachers. New digital tools and resources are consistently being invented and showcased before teachers and administrators. It can be difficult to determine which are worth implementing and how implementation should take place.

The Coaching CPR Model addresses such quandaries by facilitating collaborative coaching endeavors that begin with the end in mind. Desired outcomes receive primary focus as teachers join forces with quality coaches to determine the standards and learning goals. Together, they then work backward to outline the instructional plans.

Throughout this process, coaches must help teachers steer clear of the temptation to integrate technology simply for the sake of sprinkling in entertaining shiny new toys. Digital tools and resources often heighten student engagement and enthusiasm, but entertainment should never be the highest aim.

Technology holds tremendous potential for enhancing adventures in learning through offering meaningful, hands-on experiences with content. Yet content must always remain king, and wise coaches and teachers keep their sights fixed on the ultimate destination of student learning and the ability to transfer their learning to real-world situations.

REFERENCES

Covey, S. R. (1989). *The 7 habits of highly effective people: Restoring the character ethic*. New York, NY: Free Press.
McTighe, J., & Wiggins, G. (2012). *The Understanding by Design framework*. Alexandria, VA: ASCD. Retrieved from https://files.ascd.org/staticfiles/ascd/pdf/siteASCD/publications/UbD_WhitePaper0312.pdf
Sinek, S. (2011). *Start with why*. Harlow, UK: Penguin.

Chapter Six

The Life-Giving Power of Purposeful Pedagogy

> *"It is the supreme art of the teacher to awaken joy in creative expression and knowledge."* —Albert Einstein

In the field of education, there is no shortage of buzzwords. Some educators and educational leaders enjoy sprinkling these common terms into conversations because they may carry added weight and tend to produce a certain type of reaction. Others cringe at the sound of these same words, weary of the fleeting nature of many such buzzwords. Without common definitions, educational jargon may seem like little more than white noise.

"Pedagogy" is one such term frequently used in educational settings over the years. Although oft-repeated, pedagogy is much more than a popular buzzword. In fact, purposeful pedagogy has the power to indelibly shape nearly every aspect of students' learning experiences. In the words of Merriam-Webster, pedagogy is the "art, science, or profession of teaching." This simple definition encompasses countless facets of teaching. In fact, pedagogical considerations entail many moving parts, including teaching strategies, assessment, and feedback.

Pedagogy is sometimes confused with curriculum. While "curriculum" refers to what is being taught, "pedagogy" describes the teaching methods used. Pedagogy is shaped by a teacher's perspectives regarding the ways in which learning should, and actually does, happen.

Effective pedagogy necessitates consequential interactions and even mutual respect between educators and learners.

Ultimately, pedagogy should serve as a vehicle by which students build upon prior learning experiences, acquiring skills that will be applicable beyond the classroom setting. For this to occur, teachers must present content in a relevant manner, corresponding with learners' needs and interests. Pedagogy is naturally impacted by an educator's personal academic experiences as a student. However, successful pedagogical methods align with the context in which learning occurs.

Effective coaches transition teachers from simply using technology to transforming the learning as a result of technology use. In the Coaching CPR Model, the *P* represents the importance of pedagogically sound coaching practices. The remainder of this chapter highlights various pedagogical frameworks and considerations, as well as ways in which collegial coaches support solid, applicable, and transformative instructional practices.

THE TPACK FRAMEWORK

The previous chapter overviewed a number of content focused methods, and the TPACK framework (Herring, Koehler, & Mishra, 2016) fundamentally interconnects content and pedagogical facets of teaching and learning, aligning them with technology integration as well. This method tackles the intricate relationship between three basic types of knowledge: content (CK), pedagogy (PK), and technology (TK).

Rather than focusing on these three forms of knowledge separately, the TPACK framework accentuates the varieties of knowledge that reside at the intersections between the three basic types: pedagogical content knowledge (PCK), technological content knowledge (TCK), technological pedagogical knowledge (TPK), and technological pedagogical content knowledge (TPACK).

Successful technology implementation requires effective pedagogical practices to convey essential content knowledge. Skilled collegial coaches support teachers in attending to the interplay between these forms of knowledge—a dynamic that varies from situation to situation. Individual students, unique teachers, differing developmental levels, shifting school settings, diverse demographics, and countless other factors guarantee that each circumstance will be unique. No one amalgamation of content, pedagogy, and technology will effectively serve students in every context.

The following provides an overview of these various knowledge types, assembled by Dr. Matthew J. Koehler (2012), one of the original developers of this enduring framework:

- Content Knowledge (CK): "Teachers' knowledge about the subject matter to be learned or taught. The content to be covered in middle school science or history is different from the content to be covered in an undergraduate course on art appreciation or a graduate seminar on astrophysics. . . . As Shulman (1986) noted, this knowledge would include knowledge of concepts, theories, ideas, organizational frameworks, knowledge of evidence and proof, as well as established practices and approaches toward developing such knowledge" (Koehler & Mishra, 2009).
- Pedagogical Knowledge (PK): "Teachers' deep knowledge about the processes and practices or methods of teaching and learning. They encompass, among other things, overall educational purposes, values, and aims. This generic form of knowledge applies to understanding how students learn, general classroom management skills, lesson planning, and student assessment." (Koehler & Mishra, 2009).
- Technology Knowledge (TK): Knowledge about integrating technological tools and resources. This encompasses a broad enough understanding of technology that it can be applied in professional settings as well as in day-to-day life. This also entails recognition of when digital tools and resources can support or inhibit accomplishing set goals, as well as continued adaptation to as technological innovations occur (Koehler & Mishra, 2009).
- Pedagogical Content Knowledge (PCK): "Consistent with and similar to Shulman's idea of knowledge of pedagogy that is applicable to the teaching of specific content. Central to Shulman's conceptualization of PCK is the notion of the transformation of the subject matter for teaching. Specifically, according to Shulman (1986), this transformation occurs as the teacher interprets the subject matter, finds multiple ways to represent it, and adapts and tailors the instructional materials to alternative conceptions and students' prior knowledge. PCK covers the core business of teaching, learning, curriculum, assessment and reporting, such as the conditions that promote learning

and the links among curriculum, assessment, and pedagogy" (Koehler & Mishra, 2009).
- Technological Content Knowledge (TCK): "An understanding of the manner in which technology and content influence and constrain one another. Teachers need to master more than the subject matter they teach; they must also have a deep understanding of the manner in which the subject matter (or the kinds of representations that can be constructed) can be changed by the application of particular technologies. Teachers need to understand which specific technologies are best suited for addressing subject-matter learning in their domains and how the content dictates or perhaps even changes the technology—or vice versa" (Koehler & Mishra, 2009).
- Technological Pedagogical Knowledge (TPK): "An understanding of how teaching and learning can change when particular technologies are used in particular ways. This includes knowing the pedagogical affordances and constraints of a range of technological tools as they relate to disciplinarily and developmentally appropriate pedagogical designs and strategies" (Koehler & Mishra, 2009).
- Technological Pedagogical Content Knowledge (TPACK): "Underlying truly meaningful and deeply skilled teaching with technology, TPACK is different from knowledge of all three concepts individually. Instead, TPACK is the basis of effective teaching with technology, requiring an understanding of the representation of concepts using technologies; pedagogical techniques that use technologies in constructive ways to teach content; knowledge of what makes concepts difficult or easy to learn and how technology can help redress some of the problems that students face; knowledge of students' prior knowledge and theories of epistemology; and knowledge of how technologies can be used to build on existing knowledge to develop new epistemologies or strengthen old ones" (Koehler & Mishra, 2009).

THE SAMR MODEL

Another key factor in the success of the Coaching CPR Model is the ability to differentiate the coaching to meet each teachers' needs while moving them from substitution (in the SAMR Model) to augmentation, to modification, and finally to redefinition (Keene, 2015). The SAMR Model is an instructional framework developed by Dr. Ruben Puentedura. This model classifies four varying degrees of instructional technology incorporation: namely, substitution, augmentation, modification, and redefinition.

The SAMR Model was designed to provide a shared language across instructional contexts as teachers endeavor to create meaningful learning experiences incorporating innovative digital tools and resources. In this model, substitution and augmentation represent the "Enhancement" steps, while modification and redefinition embody "Transformation" steps. The difference between enhancement and transformation might be likened to the processes of creating a paint-by-number portrait versus creating an entirely new painting on a blank canvas.

The following section includes additional descriptions of the various phases of the SAMR model, along with examples:

- Substitution: At this phase, digital tools and resources are directly substituted for more traditional tools and resources. This phase entails a simple, direct replacement. For example, a teacher might direct students to use Google Earth to locate an unfamiliar place rather than using a paper map. In this step, it is important that educators supported by skilled collegial coaches determine potential benefits of substituting traditional tools and resources for technology. Even in the current digital age, students might be better served in some circumstances by using more traditional methods.
- Augmentation: At this phase, digital tools and resources are directly replaced by more traditional tools and resources, but now with notable enhancements. In this scenario, teachers should collaborate with coaches to decipher whether technology integration will enrich students' productivity and learning potential in significant ways. For instance, rather than writing an essay using paper and pencil, an educator might ask students to compose the essay in Microsoft Word or Google Docs so they will have access to various formatting options as well as embedded tools such as a dictionary, thesaurus, spell check, grammatical recommendations, and so on.
- Modification: In this stage, teachers transition learning experiences from enhancement to transformation. Rather than replacement or enrichment, modification entails an alteration to the design of the unit or lesson. Here, teachers supported by coaches must consider whether the integration of digital tools and resources significantly changes the task at hand. For example, rather than designing an "All

About Me" poster using chart paper and markers, students might be asked to use a digital storytelling tool, such as Little Bird Tales or Storybird, to create a mini biography that includes digital photographs from their lives, narration, and a musical background to set the tone for the story.
- Redefinition: The final stage of the SAMR model exemplifies the pinnacle of transformative educational technology use. In this case, educators should work with collegial coaches to determine if the integration of digital tools and/or resources redefines a traditional activity in ways not feasible without this technology, providing a novel learning experience. For instance, students might collaboratively create screencasts explaining various scientific theories. They could then post these screencasts to a website to be shared with students in other schools across the country as an educational tool.

Although educators and educational leaders frequently consider and discuss strategies for incorporating technology into lessons, it is difficult for many to determine whether this is taking place in meaningful ways. For example, simply substituting a digital book for a textbook is not enough to truly impact student learning. It is crucial that teachers purposefully incorporate digital tools and resources into instruction rather than haphazardly doing so for technology's sake.

This is an area in which quality coaches may be tremendously helpful. They can support teachers in remembering that the SAMR Model represents a spectrum. In some circumstances, substitution may be the most effective option. However, if a teacher's instructional style consists entirely of digitizing tools and resources without actually enhancing them, it might be helpful to consider the reasons for incorporating technology at all. Squeezing digital tools and resources into outdated activities will not significantly advance learners' acquisition of knowledge and skills. However, intentionally transforming the essence of these activities to tap into the skills students will need in the future will meaningfully impact learning for the better.

CLASSROOM INSTRUCTION THAT WORKS

As a means of classifying instructional strategies that have had the greatest impact on student achievement, the researchers of Mid-continent Research for Education and Learning (McREL) investigated and synthesized results from more than one hundred studies on instruction spanning more than thirty years. Their evaluation led to the formation of the following categories of instructional strategies for impacting achievement for all students, in every subject area, and at all grade levels:

- Note taking and summarizing
- Identify similarities and differences
- Reinforcing effort and providing recognition
- Homework and practice
- Cooperative learning
- Nonlinguistic representations
- Setting objectives and giving feedback
- Generating hypotheses
- Cues, questions, and advance organizers

In 2001, Robert J. Marzano, Debra J. Pickering, and Jane E. Pollock authored the timeless guidebook *Classroom Instruction That Works: Research-Based Strategies for Increasing Student Achievement*. Their work provides an overview of the research and theory supporting the classifications of instructional strategies first identified in the 1998 McREL report. Furthermore, the authors provide specific examples, recommendations for day-to-day practice, and guidance for instructional planning.

TECHNOLOGY'S ROLE WITHIN THESE FRAMEWORKS

When technology is used as a resource within the aforementioned instructional design frameworks, opportunities abound for its meaningful integration. Quality coaches support teachers in meaningfully applying digital tools and resources to these models. Each model offers educators and their coaches a clear-cut structure for evaluating technology's place within curricular and instructional development.

Rather than merely sprinkling technology into instructional practices because it seems new or exciting, teachers must first develop a clear understanding of the goals and objectives upon which units and lessons will be built. Working with a collegial coach, they can then identify specific ways digital tools and resources might support students in achieving those goals and objectives.

For example, technology may be employed by educators to augment instruction through video resources and presentations that deliver content through multiple modalities to support both auditory and visual learners. Technology provides teachers with strategies to demonstrate content through diverse media formats, including text, audio content, videos, hands-on modeling, and countless other applications.

Students may use digital tools and resources to give and receive feedback regarding content knowledge using adaptive learning techniques such as games and simulations. Resources like these provide students with the opportunity to independently apply new knowledge and skills in innovative ways. Some technologies even provide individualized feedback on content acquisition, differentiated to meet each student's needs. The following examples also address various tiers of Bloom's taxonomy, which is discussed more fully in chapter 5:

- Online quizzes and learning games give students the chance to test their *remembering* and *understanding* using interactive technology. For example, Quizlet (http://www.Quizlet.com) provides online flashcards and assessments that provide instantaneous feedback regarding content knowledge. Students can play online games aligned with the concepts presented in class to build their acquisition of new concepts.

Figure 6.1. Quizlet

- Technology simulations offer students experience in *applying*, *analyzing*, and *evaluating* the intersections of various content elements, encouraging them to draw their own original conclusions. The following examples feature educational simulations across content areas and developmental levels:

  - Science Simulations: The University of Colorado's PhET is an interactive resource that offers more than 200 million science-related simulations that apply to all instruction levels (http://phet.colorado.edu/en/teaching-resources/browse-activities).

Figure 6.2. PHET Interactive Simulations

- Social Studies Simulations: Through historical analogy simulation games, the everyday experiences of today's high school students are compared to historical events (https://prezi.com/jlhpamnnvmy1/causes-of-the-american-revolution-analogies/).

Figure 6.3. Causes of the American Revolution Analogies

- Mathematical Simulations: The University of Colorado's PhET also offers interactive mathematical simulations for every developmental level (https://phet.colorado.edu/en/simulations/filter?subjects=math&type=html&sort=alpha&view=grid).

Figure 6.4. PHET Interactive Simulations, Math

- The interactive technology games warehouse website (http://interactivesites.weebly.com/) contains an array of games and simulations to support students not only in augmenting their content knowledge but also with *applying* and *analyzing* the knowledge they have gained.

Figure 6.5. Interactive Sites for Education

Additionally, technology allows students to demonstrate their learning and apply new knowledge and skills to other learning situations. Web authoring tools, animation tools, presentation tools, and video creation tools can prove useful in other settings as well. These design tools provide students as well as their teachers opportunities through which to *create* and communicate content learned.

- Vocaroo (http://vocaroo.com/) and VoiceThread (http://voicethread.com/) are two examples of a variety of easily accessible, student-friendly tools for creating podcasts.

Figure 6.6. Vocaroo

Figure 6.7. VoiceThread

- Kidblog (http://kidblog.org/home/) offers learners the ability to publish blog posts in audio form, which is especially helpful for younger learners as they are developing their reading and writing skills.

Figure 6.8. Kidblog

- Digital stories tools such as Little Bird Tales (https://littlebirdtales.com/) and Storybird (http://www.storybird.com/) provide students with opportunities to create multimedia stories complete with illustrations, narration, text, music, text, and video content.

Figure 6.9. Little Bird Tales

Figure 6.10. Storybird

ESSENTIAL FACTORS TO CONSIDER WHEN PLANNING TECHNOLOGY INTEGRATION

Insightful individuals appreciate the importance of effective planning. Abraham Lincoln once declared, "Give me six hours to chop down a tree, and I will spend the first four sharpening the axe." "Sharpening the axe," so to speak, is among the greatest predictors of success for classroom technology integration. In many cases, the thought of trying out an innovative new tool or resource among twenty or more students may feel somewhat daunting. However, this prospect seems more doable with well-laid plans.

One of the most critical questions as a basis for planning is, "Will the technology integration primarily be directed by the teacher or by the students?" Insightful educators appreciate the potential of purposefully integrated technology to shift the teacher's role from "sage on the stage" to "guide on the side." When thoughtfully and meaningfully implemented, digital tools and resources hold the potential to empower a shift from the educator as a disseminator of content knowledge to a facilitator of authentic learning. Skilled collegial coaches support teachers in using solid pedagogical frameworks such as those previously mentioned to make this dream a reality.

When planning for technology integration, teachers must work with their coaches to consider the context in which digital tools and resources will be used. For example, they should contemplate such questions as the following:

- Will digital tools and resources be used in a setting in which students will be required to view teacher-created videos or other resources at home?
- Will technology be frequently accessed in a whole-group setting, such as via an interactive whiteboard?
- Will students work independently or in a more collaborative group format?
- If collaboration will occur, will this be in face-to-face settings, or will learners communicate in an online context?
- What type or types of devices will students use for learning? Will they have access to mobile devices such as smartphones, tablets, laptops, or a combination of these options?
- How will possible applications of various digital tools align with the school's or district's acceptable use policy?

- Will students be accessing downloaded apps? If so, how will they keep up with updates, and how will transferring work from devices at school to home (and back) be handled?
- How many days, weeks, or months will each unit and the corresponding lessons last?
- How much work will be accomplished at school and how much will be completed from home?
- What other learning activities might eventually need to be reduced or removed altogether in order to provide time to reach the end goals of this project?

Although the extent of questions for consideration in instructional planning might seem overwhelming, excellent collegial coaches support coached teachers in reflectively contemplating and formulating answers for each consideration. They lighten the load for teachers by serving as a sounding board and source of insight, from the initial stages of planning to each project's successful completion.

ESSENTIAL IDEAS TO REMEMBER

Rather than beginning with a focus on the technology available, impactful pedagogical endeavors focus on the most applicable strategies for engaging learners with the content knowledge. Instructional activities should be designed to support and engage students in a combination of learning tasks incorporating digital tools to learn *with* rather than *from*. Today's teachers should demonstrate not only knowledge of content but also knowledge of pedagogy and technology, and educators possessing this amalgamation of expertise are few and far between.

Successful coaches support their coached teachers in identifying impactful instructional strategies that can be incorporated with minimal stress and maximum student success. They guide colleagues in seamlessly integrating proven pedagogical methods to covey content knowledge, even before considering which technological tools should be applied. Beginning with the end in mind, they inspire the educators they serve to implement technology purposefully, when applicable. In this way, they bring added meaning to learning experiences for teachers and students alike, representing a priceless asset within educational contexts.

REFERENCES

Herring, M. C., Koehler, M. J., & Mishra, P. (2016). *Handbook of technological pedagogical content knowledge (TPACK) for educators* (2nd ed.). New York, NY: Routledge.

Keene, K. (2015, March 28) *Coaching teachers toward effective technology use: SAMR and TPACK*. Retrieved from http://www.teachintechgal.com/single-post/2015/05/28/Coaching-Teachers-Toward-Effective-Technology-Use-SAMR-TPACK

Koehler, M. J. (2012, September 24). *TPACK explained*. Retrieved from https://mattkoehler.com/tpack2/tpack-explained/

Koehler, M. J., & Mishra, P. (2009). What is technological pedagogical content knowledge? *Contemporary Issues in Technology and Teacher Education, 9*(1), 60–70.

Marzano, R. J., Pickering, D., & Pollock, J. E. (2001). *Classroom instruction that works: Research-based strategies for increasing student achievement*. Alexandria, VA: Association for Supervision and Curriculum Development.

Shulman, L. S. (1986). Those who understand: Knowledge growth in teaching. *Educational Researcher, 15*(2), 4–14.

Chapter Seven

Reviving Learning through Authentic Assessment

"If you always do what you've always done, you'll always get what you've always got." —Henry Ford

Within any professional setting, individuals typically fall into one of two categories: task focused or results oriented. Task-focused people primarily work to complete duties in a timely manner, often developing strategic processes to help them fulfill responsibilities efficiently. They accomplish quality work daily and are usually highly motivated individuals. When new opportunities arise to advance their organization, they diligently endeavor to complete step after step toward this goal. On the other hand, results-oriented individuals remain driven by the end goals they have set. They first and foremost concentrate on achieving their identified purposes rather, devoting less of their focus to routine daily procedures.

Results-oriented people often become leaders within their organization, whether through formal promotion or through less formal interactions with those around them. Such leaders naturally inspire others within their organization to approach their work with the sense of importance that ultimately makes for more fruitful workplaces. Members of results-oriented teams share a strong sense of common vision and mission, and this helps them to work more diligently toward the execution of tasks needed to achieve desired goals.

Effective results-oriented leaders play a part in building organizations that thrive as they cultivate strong relationships along colleagues. Relationships built upon trust and mutual respect represent a foundational aspect of bringing others into a shared vision and mission. Leaders who focus on result often remain open-minded and demonstrate flexibility in their approaches to completing tasks, as long as the ultimate goal remains in sight. Rather than micromanaging, they place their confidence in colleagues who share a common vision and mission, trusting them to creatively formulate strategies and solutions for achieving set goals.

The same principles hold true for collegial coaches in educational settings. Coaches who guide coached teachers in first identifying desired results and encourage them to "keep their eyes on the prize" every step of the way ultimately empower coachees to engage in more purposeful, fulfilling, and successful teaching endeavors. Similarly, educators who support their students in focusing first upon the "why" and beginning with the end in mind, as described in greater depth in chapter 5, find that students enjoy more purposeful and fulfilling learning endeavors.

In the words of William Arthur Ward, an American motivational writer, "The mediocre teacher tells. The good teacher explains. The superior teacher demonstrates. The great teacher inspires." Great teachers inspire through creating opportunities for students to discover profound purpose in their learning endeavors. Rather than first focusing on the tasks that need to be accomplished, they provide space for reflecting upon results worth working toward—results that will ultimately impact learners' lives in meaningful ways.

This line of reasoning illuminates why the R in the Coaching CPR Model is incredibly significant. Results-based coaches support coached teachers in distinguishing desired goals from the outset, working with them to create purposeful plans for achieving these goals. This models the process educators should also take as they facilitate impactful learning endeavors for their students.

The remainder of this chapter focuses upon the profound impact that results-based coaching methods ultimately have upon student learning experiences. As coaches support teachers in developing authentic learning endeavors, students receive memorable, applicable academic experiences that transfer to the world beyond the walls of the classroom.

THE FORMULA FOR MEANINGFUL LEARNING

Effective collegial coaches realize that students naturally grow increasingly motivated to learn when teachers make learning applicable to life beyond the school setting. They do this by offering them real-world problems to solve, giving them opportunities to present solutions to various audiences, and designing assessment endeavors that apply to the everyday lives of learners. This method is summed up in an innovative formula for meaningful learning: authentic issues + authentic audiences + authentic assessment = authentic learning experiences.

Many educational environments embrace a preoccupation with possessing the "latest and greatest" digital tools and resources. However, technology should never be the focus of instructional planning. Effective teaching in the digital age does not involve using devices as expensive replacements for worksheets or allowing tools to drive educational activities. In fact, insightful coaches and coached teachers realize that technology does not need to be crammed into every lesson simply for the sake of including it. Instead, assessment endeavors should find their basis in empowering students to develop the knowledge and skills they will need in future professional settings. Digital tools and resources should simply be used to enhance student learning experiences.

Today's educators must remain mindful of the fact that they are preparing learners for jobs that might not even exist at this point. According to a report published by Dell Technologies and the Institute for the Future (2018), 85 percent of the jobs that will exist in 2030 have not even been invented yet. Although teachers in today's classrooms might not be able to predict what types of professions their students will pursue in the future, they can help them develop the skills they will need to successfully encounter any job opportunity—even those that have not yet been invented!

Teachers in today's world are charged with the task of helping students dive into the DEEP end of learning experiences, supporting them as they *d*iscover, *e*ngage, *e*xperiment, and *p*roduce. Rather than jumping from digital tool to digital tool, they should focus on content first, reflecting upon what they ultimately want students to know or be able to achieve. They must allow curriculum to drive technology integration, and not vice versa, identifying tools that will help students delve deeper into learning. Insightful collegial coaches support teachers in these endeavors.

In a white paper overviewing new pedagogies for deep learning, Fullan and Scott (2014) introduced the concept of "Six Cs" of learning in the digital age, providing the following descriptions:

- Character: "Qualities of the individual essential for being personally effective in a complex world, including grit, tenacity, perseverance, resilience, reliability, and honesty"
- Citizenship: "Thinking like global citizens, considering global issues based on a deep understanding of diverse values with genuine interest in engaging with others to solve complex problems that impact human and environmental sustainability"
- Collaboration: "The capacity to work interdependently and synergistically in teams with strong interpersonal and team-related skills including effective management of team dynamics, making substantive decisions together, and learning from and contributing to the learning of others"
- Communication: "Mastery of three fluencies: digital, writing, and speaking tailored for a range of audiences"
- Creativity: "Having an 'entrepreneurial eye' for economic and social opportunities, asking the right questions to generate novel ideas, and demonstrating leadership to pursue those ideas into practice"
- Critical Thinking: "Critically evaluating information and arguments, seeing patterns and connections, construction meaningful knowledge and applying it in the real world" (pp. 6–7)

Effective technology integration is an instructional decision that includes thoughtful planning on the part of teachers and their coaches as they seek to incorporate these skills—skills that will be applicable to students' future life endeavors, no matter the professional paths they pursue. This type of instructional design frequently involves a paradigm shift. Successful coaches support teachers in shifting their perceptions of students from consumers of information to creators of new learning experiences.

Rather than focusing on using an interactive screen and having a device in every hand, teachers should be encouraged to provide opportunities for students to collaborate with classmates in solving real-world problems. Furthermore, they should facilitate experiences in which students create innovative products to share beyond the walls of their classroom.

This paradigm shift requires teachers to transition from being the "sage of the stage" to the "guide on the side." For many educators who were taught using more traditional methods from their early childhood through their years in higher education, this may present an incredibly challenging transition. The "sage on the stage" teaching style may be the one they feel most comfortable using, simply because this is the method with which they are most familiar. Yet skilled coaches empower more traditionally minded teachers to adopt innovative strategies through shoulder-to-shoulder guidance and active modeling in classroom contexts.

Impactful teaching in today's world focuses on making learning experiences authentic or more meaningful for students. When students are given opportunities to envision how they might use targeted knowledge and skills within a variety of future contexts, they will more naturally remain engaged and motivated throughout the learning process, ultimately make learning more memorable!

TACKLING AUTHENTIC ISSUES

Adults must engage in decision-making and problem-solving endeavors countless times throughout each day, finding resolutions for various issues in life. Yet many students struggle with this process. It could be that they are not provided with adequate opportunities to formulate decisions on their own. Students spend most of their waking hours at school, and during this highly influential time frame, they should be encouraged to confront and solve various problems.

Gerald Aungst, an expert in mathematics curriculum, digital literacy, and gifted education, as well as the author of the *Five Principles of the Modern Mathematics Classroom* (2015), outlines five steps to cultivating a problem-solving classroom culture: conjecture, communication, collaboration, chaos, and celebration. In an edWeb (2014) webinar featuring Aungst, he reveals information about problem-solving that stretches far beyond the mathematics curriculum (Devaney, 2014).

According to Aungst, "The world does not need more people who are good at math. What the world needs are more problem solvers and more innovators." Innovators do not simply accept that challenging problems are impossible to solve, even if others have stated that this is the case. In referring to the "conjecture" stage of problem-solving, Aungst explains, "It's about students, not just solving problems—it's about them looking for problems, too. . . . Innovators are looking for problems, and they try to solve them before anyone even realizes the problem exists. We need innovators" (edWed webinar, 2014).

Rather than striving to provide solutions in every situation, educators should seek to avoid ending each lesson with an answer. Instead, they should ask students what they believe the answer may be, how they arrived at this solution, and whether alternative solutions exist. Collegial coaches can support teachers in designing assessment opportunities that include chances to find problems to solve. An excellent digital tool to support opportunities for conjecture is Data.gov (http://data.gov).

Through the "communication" component of this process, students practice explaining their thought processes, thus increasing their own knowledge. Students should be able to explain potential solutions in their own words; communication is a skill that can be incorporated in every area of life, no matter what professional endeavors they pursue. Digital tools to inspire practice with effective communication include Piktochart (https://piktochart.com/) and Infogram (https://infogram.com/), as well as videos posted to YouTube or classroom blogs.

The "collaboration" element plays into countless areas of everyday life, as problem-solving in the real world so often involves collaboration with others. Through partnering together in problem-solving endeavors, students have the chance to contemplate other perspectives, engaging in reciprocal learning experiences that may ultimately impact their thinking in helpful ways. Countless digital tools and resources have been developed to support problem-solving endeavors, including cloud-based Google products such as Google Docs, Google Slides, and Google Sheets, as well as online Office 365 products such as Microsoft Word, Microsoft PowerPoint, and Microsoft Excel.

The "chaos" component of problem-solving embraces the fact that problem-solving endeavors are typically not straightforward in nature. In fact, most often, they are at least somewhat messy. Students should

Figure 7.1.   Data.gov

Figure 7.2. Piktochart

be exposed to learning endeavors that encourage them to wrestle with problems in meaningful ways, making learning situations more productive and purposeful.

Finally, the "celebration" element encompasses opportunities to highlight students' development and victories, as well as setbacks that ultimately produce new growth. As Aungst advises teachers, "It's really important that you validate effort, and not answers. . . . It's really important that we recognize that the students who start out as the smartest at the beginning of the year may not be the smartest at the end of the year." Innovative collegial coaches can support teachers in incorporating these five steps into everyday learning opportunities to cultivate problem-solving skills that will ultimately benefit students in every area of life, both currently and in the future.

Community gardens developed by students provide an excellent example of school-based problem-solving in action that may or may not involve digital tools and resources. For example, in the Houston area, Urban Harvest (https://www.urbanharvest.org/education/youth/school-partnerships/) empowers schools to plant and cultivate gardens and provides nutrition classes to explore healthy eating, native habitats, and ecosystems. This initiative bridges schools with their communities, allowing students to work collaboratively to create a positive difference. As they engage in service-based learning, students naturally solve real-world problems along the way that will ultimately impact their community for the better.

PRESENTING TO AUTHENTIC AUDIENCES

Assessment opportunities should offer students the chance to share their learning with others, thus providing them incentive to produce their very best work. When they know that people besides their teacher will be viewing and possibly even interacting with their creations, they typically discover greater purpose in their work. In an increasingly

Figure 7.3. Infogram

interconnected world, digital tools and resources make boundless opportunities available for students to share their work with real-life audiences beyond the walls of their classroom.

Paralleling the backward design framework discussed in chapter 5, the first step in finding an authentic audience for students entails identifying the desired results, carefully considering the ultimate learning goals and objectives. Next, teachers should reflect upon the form the project will take. Perhaps students will be attempting to solve an issue within their community using the concepts they are learning in social studies. Maybe they will investigate an issue surrounding current events that reflects a problem they are exploring through their history lessons. As teachers collaborate with coaches to determine the goals and objectives to address through the creation process, an appropriate intended audience will be easier to identify.

Authentic audiences should vary from project to project, providing students with opportunities to apply developing skills in the presence of different groups of people. Teachers may begin by seeking familiar audience members, such as family, friends, or others who already have an interest in students' lives. Learners might also present their creations to others within the school setting, such as students in other classes or grade levels as well as administrators or instructional support specialists. It may also be helpful to seek the support of experts in the field. For example, students working on an impressionist painting project in art class might host a gallery walk and invite a local artist to tour the exhibit.

In the *Glossary of Education Reform* (Abbott, 2014), assessment is defined as "the wide variety of methods or tools that educators use to evaluate, measure, and document the academic readiness, learning progress, skill acquisition, or educational needs of students."

Performance assessments, or "authentic assessments," involve a student-created product such as a science experiment, presentation, portfolio, multimedia piece, and the list goes on and on. Authentic assess-

Figure 7.4. Urban Harvest

ments should incorporate as many of the previously overviewed "Six Cs" as possible in order to provide students the opportunity to implement skills they will need for the future. By design, these assessments apply learning to real-life contexts or experiences. With this being the case, the finished products of these assessments may take on an infinite variety of forms.

In many cases, performance-based assessments offer more meaningful appraisals of learning for both teachers and students, as they naturally highlight strengths and weaknesses in relation to instructional design and delivery as well as resultant student learning. They provide a revealing glimpse of what learners actually know and what they can actually do, rather than simply showcasing how skillfully students can take quizzes or exams. Authentic assessments provide opportunities for learners to create novel end products, rather than simply requiring that they consume information for the purpose of regurgitating it while taking a quiz or exam.

In fact, the undergraduate and graduate education courses I have developed for my university do not include any quizzes or exams. Rather, they incorporate assessment opportunities that directly apply to students' current or future endeavors as teachers. Throughout each course, students design artifacts of learning that correlate with standards required of teachers. Students begin with the end in mind as they create digital tools and resources to be used within their classroom settings.

These current and aspiring educators design assessment pieces with purpose, motivated by the fact that their students will benefit from their efforts. As a result, their finished products showcase educational excellence, and these current and future teachers often demonstrate great excitement to share their digital portfolios filled with their artifacts of learning. In fact, students at times include a link to their portfolio in their e-mail signature or add a QR code to their résumé to point those within their professional networks to their incredible creations. Some students have even been hired or received awards or promotions as a result of their noteworthy digital portfolios.

The figure below is an exemplary portfolio created by one of my students, Veronica Velarde, toward the start of her undergraduate teacher education coursework (https://veronicavelarde.weebly.com/).

ASSESSING WITH INTENTIONALITY

The process of evaluating authentic assessment products requires that teachers determine how effectively the end results demonstrate acquired knowledge and skills. Thoughtfully designed, criteria-based rubrics allow students to determine from the outset how their work will be evaluated. This way, students—and not only their teachers—receive the chance to begin with the end in mind. Effectively constructed rubrics focus specifically and purposefully on addressing criteria for excellence, in order that students can avoid haphazardly piecing projects together. Rubrics alleviate "surprise" elements of grading, allowing students to gain advance insights into how the grading process occur.

Another advantage of incorporating rubrics involves their potential for meaningfully informing parents about the assessment process. Like students, parents typically do not appreciate surprises in the grading process. Rubrics provide heightened communication and clarity as parents review the graded assessments their children bring home. Additionally, they offer useful information that parents might discuss with students while reflecting upon their progress toward learning goals and determining potential steps for improved future assessment outcomes.

ASSESSMENT IN ACTION: RUBRIC RESOURCES TO GUIDE THE WAY

The final section of this chapter features a number of rubric creation tools that may be useful for evaluating artifacts of learning in various

Figure 7.5. Ms. Velarde's Professional Portfolio

classroom contexts. These rubrics should be tailored to align with the purposes of different academic scenarios, addressing instructional goals and objectives specific to each unit, lesson, and set of students. Excellent coaches work with teachers to locate or create rubrics tailored to fit various unique assessment experiences.

A variety of ready-made rubrics found on numerous educational websites apply to a wide range of educational environments. Among these, Kathy Schrock's site (http://www.schrockguide.net/assessment-and-rubrics.html) is brimming with expertly designed rubrics to support assessment of many different types of student products.

Figure 7.6.   Kathy Schrock's Guide to Everything: Assessment and Rubrics

For teachers desiring to create rubrics of their own, numerous sites specifically support this endeavor. Rubistar (http://rubistar.4teachers.org) offers valuable resources for educators who may not have time to develop rubrics from scratch and could benefit from a starting point. Varying templates allow teachers to incorporate precreated criteria, and all rubrics are editable so that specific goals and objectives can easily be incorporated.

Figure 7.7.   Rubistar

ESSENTIAL IDEAS TO REMEMBER

Results-based coaching methods indelibly impact student learning experiences. As coaches support teachers in developing authentic academic endeavors, students receive memorable, applicable learning experiences that transfer to the world beyond the walls of the classroom. An innovative formula for meaningful learning is: authentic issues + authentic audiences + authentic assessment = authentic learning experiences.

Quality coaches walk with teachers through every step of the process as they seek to introduce students to real-world problems to solve, provide them with the opportunity to present solutions to various audiences, and design assessment endeavors that apply to the everyday lives of learners. In this way, coaches support educators in creating learning experiences that meaningfully impact students for a lifetime.

REFERENCES

Abbott, S. (Ed.). Hidden curriculum. (2014, August 26). In S. Abbott (Ed.), *The glossary of education reform*. http://edglossary.org/hidden-curriculum

Aungst, G. (2015). *Five principles of the modern mathematics classroom: Creating a culture of innovative thinking*. Thousand Oaks, CA: Corwin.

Devaney, L. (2014, September 17). Five steps to a problem-solving classroom culture. *eSchool News*. Retrieved from https://www.eschoolnews.com/2014/09/17/problem-solving-culture-904/print/

edWeb (2014, August 20). Creating a culture of problem solving in your school or classroom. Retrieved from https://home.edweb.net/creating-culture-problem-solving-school-classroom/

Fullan, M., & Scott, G. (2014). *New pedagogies for deep learning whitepaper: Education PLUS*. Seattle, WA: Collaborative Impact SPC.

Institute for the Future (IFTF), for Dell Technologies. (2018). *Realizing 2030: A divided vision of the future: Global business leaders forecast the next era of human-machine partnerships and how they intend to prepare* [summary]. Retrieved from https://www.delltechnologies.com/content/dam/delltechnologies/assets/perspectives/2030/pdf/Realizing-2030-A-Divided-Vision-of-the-Future-Summary.pdf

Conclusion

> *"If you can't fly then run, if you can't run then walk, if you can't walk then crawl, but whatever you do, you have to keep moving forward."—*
> Martin Luther King Jr.

The Coaching CPR Method offers a vision and pathway through which educational organizations can leverage the power of collegial coaching to transform learning endeavors. As coached educators accomplish milestones of development, their confidence and excitement naturally overflows, inspiring their sharing of these successes with fellow colleagues. The enduring impacts of collegial coaching fundamentally represent a synthesis of research-based, time-proven principles of teaching and learning.

For instance, coaching involves the Vygotskian principle of the zone of proximal development. Over many years, countless educators have used this concept in their classrooms through investigating students' current levels of development and potential for growth in the future, allowing them to support each individual learner more successfully in attaining increasingly advanced concepts and skills.

This is how scaffolding impacts instructional endeavors. The zone of proximal development signifies the gap between a student's level of autonomous performance and the next level of supported performance, or what that student can accomplish with help. When using the Coaching CPR Method, collegial coaches offer the scaffolding necessary to bridge such gaps, connecting the points between a coachee's independent technology integration ability and those skills still yet to be grasped.

Along with assimilating the zone of proximal development, the Coaching CPR Method also incorporates reciprocal teaching methods, based upon Vygotsky's theories regarding the foundational role of social engagement, or dialogue, in the growth of cognition. According to this principle, thinking out loud and talking about ideas encourage enlightenment and the revision of learning, thereby improving cognition. During reciprocal instructional endeavors, the necessary guidance and feedback should be provided to facilitate impactful learning.

Ultimately, the potential for learning expands as reciprocal learning participants take turns serving as the teacher. Through the Coaching CPR Method, both the coach and the coached teacher share the responsibilities of instructor and student, thus giving both the opportunity to develop within their roles. As they think aloud and discuss insights together, powerful reciprocal learning endeavors unfold, benefitting collegial coaching participants as well as the students.

AGE IS MERELY A NUMBER

One might assume that the Coaching CPR Method targets a certain age group of teachers for technology integration support—namely, more seasoned faculty members. In reality, through my work with coaches and coached teachers over the years, it became increasingly evident that while technological operations may come more naturally to some younger teachers, those teachers may not yet possess the content or instructional expertise to leverage digital tools and resources for empowered learning experiences. Along those lines, newer faculty members may not be as confident in encouraging technology use among students in light of potential classroom management issues.

No matter the length of their teaching experience, educators of all ages can benefit from content-focused, pedagogically sound, results-based technology integration support. The Coaching CPR Method offers a supportive professional relationship through which a collegial coach offers support relating to a coached teacher's most pressing needs, and this form of individualized, targeted guidance is one factor that sets this framework apart from other, less personalized professional development experiences.

A related situation occurred with a higher education faculty member who once worked alongside me. During a meeting of faculty members from various disciples, this professor remarked that some of his fellow faculty members were banning the use of laptops in class. As one might expect, the School of Education faculty members were quite perplexed by this announcement. For some, a glaring question came to mind: Undoubtedly, students will be required to effectively use computers and various other digital tools within their professional lives. Why would someone decide to ban laptops from the very courses designed to prepare them to enter and eventually impact their professional spheres?

As this faculty member's statement was further discussed, it became clear that this prohibition of laptops stemmed from issues involving classroom management. The colleagues making this decision felt frustrated by the thought that students might make use of their laptops for activities other than recording each word their professors spoke during the course of a lecture.

Furthermore, pedagogical issues seemed to be involved. In instances when students are not invited to actively engage in learning, they will naturally find alternative means of occupying their minds. Whether engaging with social media apps, checking e-mails, or texting—or possibly, in cases where technology is forbidden, discreetly doodling in a notebook—they will find a way to fill their time. Insightful educators understand that students must be invited to engage their minds throughout each learning experience. The faculty members banning laptops, although exceptionally knowledgeable in their content area, might have benefitted from coaching to bolter engaging instructional strategies.

In cases such as this, the Coaching CPR Method offers new avenues for investigating innovative methods of engaging students. Perhaps consistent lecturing falls short of best serving the students, even in higher educational settings. It is highly possible that a simulation or game designed to augment knowledge and skills might result in greater impact than sharing an anecdote from a textbook. There is always room for improvement in teaching and learning contexts, regardless of the faculty experience or student developmental level.

Instructional coaches with content knowledge, pedagogical skill, and technological expertise will be more and more needed as technology integration grows increasingly imperative in educational contexts. This reality was never more apparent than amid the global COVID-19 pandemic, when schools around the world suddenly transitioned to fully remote learning. Those educators with mastery of not only content knowledge and pedagogical skill but also technological expertise suddenly became the most valued sources of support in their school communities.

In response to ever-shifting academic landscapes such as the world witnessed because of the pandemic, successful teachers will endeavor to plan instructional experiences that incorporate student-centered technology applications while also encouraging the construction of content knowledge. This process, of course, will fluctuate greatly from situation to situation depending upon the learners' development levels as well as their access to digital tools and resources. Collegial coaches' responsibilities and levels of support will vary greatly also.

As discussed in previous chapters, meaningful technology incorporation engages, motivates, and empowers students while helping them to gain new content-area expertise. Even considering the impact digital tools and resources may have upon learning experiences, technology is simply a tool; it is not a magic wand.

Incorporating technology does not guarantee learning for all students. Yet, when appropriate tools are strategically employed to teach content, the door of opportunity for engaging instruction and resultant learning often swings open. The art of designing lessons that meaningfully integrate technology necessitates content knowledge, pedagogical expertise, and technical skill. As collegial coaches commence their work with teachers, they must decipher each coachee's prior knowledge in relation to technology integration, subject-area content, and instructional expertise. When coaches and coached teachers collaborate from the very first step onward, both greatly benefit from this reciprocal learning process.

THE OPTIONS ARE ENDLESS

Ultimately, educational leaders must determine the type of coaching implementation best suited for their school community. For those who wish to initiate a formal coaching experience, they might opt to hire one or more qualified individuals to operate as collegial coaches. Alternatively, they might elect to begin with a less formal program, selecting faculty members already in the school setting to start a peer-focused program. While each option entails various considerations and implications, either method can be incredibly successful.

The peer-focused option comprises a more grassroots approach and can easily foster powerful ripple effects among faculty members. In this situation, coaches volunteer or are hand-picked by administrators. As they collaborate with fellow colleagues, the focus should consistently remain on teacher and student successes. Every accomplishment should be honored; as a result, each celebration will lead to increased self-confidence for the coachees.

Ripple effects represent a hallmark of successful coaching programs. Through great and small victories, coached teachers develop increasing enthusiasm regarding the results of their time and efforts invested with coaches. In turn, along with every new celebration, they often experience a heightened desire to tell their stories to others, eventually becoming informal coaches themselves.

Excellent educators understand that the excitement surrounding meaningful learning experiences typically becomes contagious, and this includes learning that occurs because of collegial coaching programs. In time, even small, less formal coaching programs may grow to be campus-wide initiatives from which all within the school community can benefit.

In some cases, school leadership may opt to implement a formal coaching program from the start. In such circumstances, collegial coaches may be interviewed and hired to support quality teaching endeavors involving technology integration. The benefits of such programs may include more formalized evaluation and reporting processes. Often in these situations, because coaching entails an official expense, an added level of accountability on the part of coaches and coachees might be involved. Programs of this nature may eventually lead to further time and effort dedicated to coaching by both coaches and coached teachers.

Because faculty members find themselves frequently pressed for time, scheduling formal meetings with coaches (especially if a single individual is coaching multiple teachers), researching strategies for support, and guiding coachees through the completion of every project may present a challenge. However, this undertaking may become more feasible when one or more people are hired to devote their time solely to the vision established on a campus for collegial coaching.

CONFIRMATION OF COLLEGIAL COACHING SUCCESS

This guidebook concludes with real-life triumphs related to collegial coaching, cultivated to inform and inspire readers as they journey toward implementing the Coaching CPR Method in their own professional contexts. Narratives such as these confirm that an investment in collegial coaching carries tremendous promise to transform a campus culture in profound and enduring ways.

Through studies conducted with my mentor, Dr. Dawn Wilson, more than sixty-five campuses have witnessed success story after success story with collegial coaching (Alaniz & Wilson, 2015). The following remarks represent various coached teachers' testimonials regarding their experience over the course of a semester:

- "My students were engaged, and authentic application and evaluation were truly happening in my classroom."
- "I am finally beginning to see how technology is not just an extra burden, but a fun and meaningful tool to help kids learn content."
- "This experience was very streamlined and well organized, making it easy to work with my coach to integrate these new tools into my classroom."
- "Technology coaching has opened my eyes to the possibility of improving my methods in the classroom. I also realize how much the students enjoy using it. Allowing students complete access for assessments is a positive change of pace from in-class paper/pencil assessments."
- "I liked the hands-on ability to see the tool in use, and then being able to practice it."

Additionally, below are several quotes from the coaches themselves regarding their experiences coaching fellow faculty members:

- "The best thing about coaching for technology integration is the fluid concept for both the mentor and coach. It allows each teacher to grow at a pace he/she is comfortable with, while challenging each in a fun and comfortable manner. Barriers are reduced and comfort levels rise, allowing creativity to bloom."
- "Technology integration does not happen from a help desk."
- "This experience also opened my eyes to how valuable collegial coaching is as compared to the traditional professional development

that teachers are required to complete today. In this process, not only does a teacher have one point of contact for questions, issues, concerns, and ideas, but they also get the chance to try things in their classroom in a real-time basis rather than having to wait until the school year starts to try something. That is not to say that the traditional professional development is a thing of the past, but it might be most appropriate when used in combination with a collegial coaching model."
- "I truly believe the coaching process is the most effective form of professional development. Every learner, no matter what age, benefits when instruction is personalized, supportive, and tailored to meet the learner's specific needs. Schools that utilize technology coaches will see an increase in teacher and student achievement in a shorter period of time than schools that simply rely on standard professional development."
- "I would recommend educators or administrators who want to increase the technology use in their school to consider using individualized coaching rather than faculty-wide professional development. There are a few individuals who will implement a new technology after brief exposure to it, but I think the majority of teachers require additional prompting and individualization before they realize how effective the technology could be in their classrooms. From my coaching experience, I learned change in an individual takes time. I think relationship, accountability, and an ability to individualize technology to fit specific personality types and content is essential for a coach."
- "In my role as instructional technologist, I have decided to drop my 'Tech Tuesdays' in lieu of more lucrative content knowledge oriented individual coaching."

ESSENTIAL IDEAS TO REMEMBER

For educators to find success through the Coaching CPR Method, they must appreciate the fact that effective coaching requires time. Coaches and coached teachers alike must be willing to dedicate the time needed to move projects to completion, achieve significant goals, and witness meaningful and enduring benefits as a result of the experience. Successful coaches and teachers carve out time to conference together for planning, conduct research, and develop instructional resources. The process will not necessarily be easy, but increased student engagement and learning are worth the investment.

Technological innovations will continue to surge, and with each new advancement, students will grow ever more fascinated by the potential technology holds for empowering creation, critical thinking, communication, collaboration, character, and citizenship. As they face an ever-evolving world, effective teachers will consistently adapt their professional strategies to reach learners at their varying points of engagement and interest. If they refuse to do so, they ultimately risk losing students altogether.

Over the past several years, many educational settings have greatly struggled with integrating technology in meaningful and effective ways, especially very recently through the movement toward remote instruction spurred by the pandemic. Sometimes, such challenges are magnified when the latest and greatest digital tools are resources are purchased in the absence of investment in the most priceless of all school resources—the human resources.

Steps should be taken to support every teacher's need to be empowered rather than overwhelmed. The Coaching CPR Model addresses this need by encouraging educators and their students to embrace the promise of effectively applied technologies, ultimately bringing profound and lasting impact within this extraordinary age of innovation.

REFERENCES

Alaniz, K., & Wilson, D. (2015). *Naturalizing digital immigrants: The power of collegial coaching for technology integration.* Lanham, MD: Rowman & Littlefield Education.

About the Author

Katie Alaniz, EdD, is a faculty member in the College of Education Behavioral Sciences at Houston Baptist University, where she also serves as director of the Center for Learning Innovations and Teaching Excellence (C-LITE) and program coordinator of the Master of Science in Learning, Technology, and Design program. As a teacher and digital learning specialist for more than a decade in both public and private schools, including her service as a digital learning specialist at River Oaks Baptist School, Dr. Alaniz guides educators as they meaningfully integrate digital tools and resources within their classrooms. Together with colleagues at HBU, Dr. Alaniz has coauthored *Naturalizing Digital Immigrants: The Power of Collegial Coaching for Technology Integration* and *Digital Media in Today's Classrooms: The Potential for Meaningful Teaching, Learning, and Assessment*. Dr. Alaniz and her husband, Steven, reside in Houston, Texas.

www.ingramcontent.com/pod-product-compliance
Lightning Source LLC
Chambersburg PA
CBHW032029230426
43671CB00005B/249